GOOGLE
Hacks Exposed

Improving Your
Rank on Google

Kevin Prag

Google Hacks Exposed – Improving your Rank on Google

Published by Global Niches LLC
Global Niches
4894 Lone Mountain Rd. #206
Las Vegas, NV 89130

Writer: Kevin Prag

ISBN: 0-9754534-1-6

Produced in the United States of America

For information such as press inquiries, licensing, author interviews or other information, please contact the publisher by email at globalniches@yahoo.com. Publisher may also be reached at the address listed above. For information on future updates and new books, please visit http://www.google-hacks.com

Table of Contents

Preface

This book was written to help understand Google better. Search results on Google have been changing over past couple of years and this book was written to show why sites are ranked high by Google and why sites are ranked low.

This book outlines some of the most common hacks that people have taken to get ranked high on Google and some less obvious ones. Some of them are hacks of the past, while others are new hacks that offer some new ideas.

The tips and hacks recommended in this book are long term hacks that should continue to work for at least the next few years or more. These hacks are tips that you can do that should improve your website rankings over a long period of time and not getting you banned by Google.

This book also details some risky hacks that may also be an option for some. Opinions are given on each of the hacks as far as the risk of each hack and whether the hack is worth considering.

The sources used for this book have been included at the bottom of each section for your convenience.

Attempts have been made to make hacks visibly available with image screenshots of the hack. This was not always possible because the words in the search results are not deemed appropriate for all audiences. In such cases, the specific search results are not displayed, but the description of the hack is explained.

This book has been proofread several times to eliminate misspellings and miswordings. You may still find some grammatical errors such the occasional sentence fragment or run on sentence; however, this was not intended. Regardless, this book was written to be easy to read by most and should be very helpful.

I hope you enjoy this book and hope it helps you improve your search rank in Google and other search engines.

Introduction – History of Google

Before jumping into the hacks, it is first important that we understand the history of Google. Google was formed in 1995 by two Stanford University graduate students: Larry Page and Sergey Brin.

The idea was to create a better search engine than the competition. By 1998, they had a beta version of Google running. It had become very popular and had impressed some investors. One such investor was one of the founders of Sun Microsystems, Andy Bechtolsheim. He wrote Google a check for $100,000 after seeing the search engine in action and the company started to take off.

By September 1998, Google opened its door in Menlo Park, California. Its first employee was hired and Google was generating 10,000 search queries a day.

Google quickly outgrew its office and started getting lots of media attention. This drew the attention of two major venture capital firms in Silicon Valley, Sequoia Capital and Kleiner Perkins Caufield & Buyers. They put $25 million into Google.

On September 21, 1999 the beta label came off the website. Shortly after came the pay per search word option, Google Adwords and late 2000, Google introduced Google toolbar.

Google's success was further improved by a deal with Yahoo to provide search engine technology for its site. This brought Google to public eye as one of the most popular search engines around.

As a result of its immense success, Google has received awards for the best search engine by many different sources such as Yahoolife, and Search Engine Watch.

Search the web using Google!

[10 results ▾] [Google Search] [I'm feeling lucky]

Index contains ~25 million pages (soon to be much bigger)

About Google!

Stanford Search   Linux Search

Get Google! updates monthly!

[your e-mail   ] [Subscribe] Archive

This picture is an actual screenshot of Google's website from November 1998.

The Technology behind Google

Google is made up of thousands of computer systems which work together with one another in clusters. Each system is similar to what an ordinary desktop computer might look like except that it is loaded with specialized software and doesn't have some of the hardware regular PCs have such as CD-ROM and graphics cards.

The software operating system that Google used initially was UNIX based. Google chose a special variant of UNIX called BSD. Now they are using Linux which is a variant of UNIX which is more user friendly. Google then chose a stripped down version of Redhat Linux. Linux is available for free download off of the internet. Support is available for paid versions. As a goodwill gesture, Google purchased around fifty copies of Redhat from Redhat.

Google Hacks Exposed

Most of the support for Linux is provided by the open source community and by Google employees.

Some have said that Google has the largest number of Linux servers in the world. That has yet to be confirmed, but the number of servers in use is estimated at around 40-80 thousand servers.

Estimates have also been made as to how Google stacks up as a supercomputer. When adding all of the computing power between servers, estimates are that Google has between 253 and 316 teraflops. This would put Google into the list for the top supercomputers.

The reason for using Linux for the operating system for Google is that it is low cost, customizable and stable. By choosing thousands of low cost PC's instead of large mainframes, Google has the lowest cost per performance and few single points of failure.

If one server fails, it is no big loss to Google. Other systems can pick up the load and the end user may not even notice anything. With a large supercomputer or mainframe, the cost per performance is higher and if the server goes down it is much more of an effect on business that if one tiny server goes down.

Google uses fault tolerant systems with many systems carrying the information of other systems in case one system goes down there is a backup of that data.

The hard drives that Google uses are basic IDE or ATA based hard drives. These are the same types of hard drives used in your home PC's. They offer a lower cost per GB than alternative technologies such as SCSI or firewire based hard drives.

Google has global hardware based load balancers. As the traffic comes in, the load balancer decides which datacenter to forward the traffic to. Then that datacenter will send traffic to various computers within the datacenter.

Each Google datacenter is made up of hundreds or thousands of Google computer servers. Google has datacenters across the world which it has servers in.

The links below will give you some further info as to the technology behind Google.

http://technetcast.ddj.com/tnc_play_stream.html?stream_id=420

http://www.internetweek.com/lead/lead060100.htm
http://www.tnl.net/blog/entry/How_many_Google_machines

http://www.hpworld.com/hpworldnews/hpw009/02nt.html
http://www.google.com/technology/pigeonrank.html

Search Engine Evolution

The competition in the search engine business has changed quite a bit since 1998. During that time, companies such as Lycos, AltaVista, Go, MSN, Excite, Infoseek, and Hotbot were all providing search engine services.

They all allowed free submissions until after the dot com bubble in the year 2000. At this point, most started charging people for URL submissions. By only allowing paid submissions, the competition had made search results more commercial and less relevant for many internet surfers.

Google was one of the exceptions to this and did not charge and does not charge to this day for submitting websites to its search engine. By not charging for submissions, Google set itself apart from the competition in that it would not sacrifice the quality of its search results for money.

Instead of charging for paid search engine submission, Google started Adwords program which allows people to bid on keywords and have a special section of the search engine results page dedicated for "sponsored listings."

Even with paid submissions many of the search engines could not make enough money to continue. Many merged with other companies and many stopped developing their own search engine and started using search engine technology from other companies. Many of the search engine names still exist, but the underlying search technology is now much different.

Alltheweb.com (fast.com), altavista.com, yahoo.com are now all powered by Yahoo's search engine technology. Yahoo developed their own search engine after it cancelled its contract with Google. One of the problems Yahoo was having was, they were paying for search engine technology from Google and many people were starting to go directly to Google instead of Yahoo for internet searches.

http://www.google.com/corporate/history.html

Designing the ideal search engine

Before we dig into the tricks of getting ranked high on Google, we must dive into what the founders of Google must have been thinking when they created Google.

As mentioned, Google had plenty of competition when they entered the market. Inkotomi was providing search engine technology for many of the search engines on the internet. Many new search engines were getting started and everyone was thriving on venture capital funds.

However, spamming and search engine tricks were starting to get more prevalent. Problems with lots of search results during this time were that cheaters were doing all sorts of tricks to get listed high. They were putting lots of keywords and text in meta-tags to make web pages show up better. They were using alt tags on images with lots of keywords and burying hidden text into pages loaded with keywords.

Keywords, keywords, keywords were the most important thing during this time. The quality of a site didn't play a role in getting ranked highly during this time; it was simply the stuffing of keywords throughout pages that helped people get ranked high.

So, when Google entered the market, they would need to find ways of dealing with spammers. Search engine results with Google were to be based on the quality of pages and not on tricks. More popular sites were to be ranked higher than those that were not as popular.

How did Google achieve this?

Google set a new precedent by ignoring Meta tags. Meta-tags were so abused during this time that ignoring them instantly gave Google more relevant search results. Page title and body text played a much more important role with Google. Also page links from outside sources and internal links became important with Google.

Public popularity became an important way of ranking sites. Google expected popular sites to have others linking to them. And, the more sites others have linking to them, the higher up their site should be in the ranking. This was pretty much a new thing at the time and made it harder to cheat.

Another common trick of the early years was search engine cloaking. In order to get listed high, lots of keywords and text were important. Unfortunately, web pages were often unreadable and ugly in order to get ranked high. To get around this, people started cloaking. This means, you let the search engine spider see only the keyword pages by finding out the IP addresses of the search engine robots and only letting them see these pages.

Search engines have many servers and computers connected to internet. In order to get a webpage listed on a search engine, it must be submitted to the search engine. After this is done, the search engine computers must look at website to see what is on the page and how it will be ranked. This is called spidering and the search engines computers are referred to as "spiders" or "bots." Each one of these systems has a unique identifier or IP address. This is a number that looks something like 66.94.230.32.

The way cloaking works is to determine the IP addresses of all of the bots and show them a different webpage than your human website visitors. The search bots get to see ugly keyword pages, while your human visitors see only your pretty webpage.

The problem with this is that it is another form of deception to the viewer and most search engines will ban websites that cloak. Google has servers scattered throughout the US on many different IP addresses and it becomes very difficult to keep up with all the Google IP addresses.

Some people and search engine optimization have all sorts of ways that they state justifies the use of cloaking. Some may say that they are making it easier for human visitors by only showing them easy to read, pretty pages. Others may state that cloaking done the right way is effective and ethical. Regardless of their arguments it is still deception and they are not being honest with Google. And, when their website domain name is banned, Google is not going to be receptive to their arguments.

While designing Google, the founders must have been thinking about what ideal search engine would be like.

The ideal search engine allows the webmaster to build a website without having to think about search engines and search engine tricks. Of course this would be the ideal search engine. In its current stage, no computer based search engine can do this. An example would be if you created an entire webpage in Photoshop, this would severely limit page indexing because of the lack of text on the page.

On the search results for you site, Google typically pulls text from the title and body of your webpage and puts it in your description for the search results. No text on the site means no text in search results and probably a poor rating. Without keywords, Google has no way of knowing how to rank your website.

The ideal search engine should not allow cheaters to get listed very high for a long period of time. This is usually true on Google. For a while, some cheaters were dominating certain keywords for probably six months or more. Then, when Google modified their algorithm in November 2003, most of them disappeared from the search results on Google.

Google Employees Speak

As a result of Google's incredible popularity, some interviews have been done by the founders of Google and some of its top employees. Below are some links of interviews with Google employees. Some of them are text base interviews while others are audio based interviews.

5-11-2004 Google CTO Google's man behind the curtain
http://www.zdnet.com.au/insight/hardware/0,39023759,3914712 0,00.htm

5-3-2004 Google Founder Google's Goal: "Understand Everything"
http://www.businessweek.com/magazine/content/04_18/b388101 0_mz001.htm

10-14-2003 Founders on NPR Fresh Air
http://freshair.npr.org/day_fa.jhtml?display=day&todayDate=10/1 4/2003

July 2002 Google's CTO Does Google penalize sites that are virtual hosted? Does Google use traffic analysis for its ranking algorithm? What technology is used to operate Google?
http://interviews.slashdot.org/article.pl?sid=02/07/03/1352239

February 2002 Google Software Engineer. Google Globalization Specialist Does Google use META keywords? Does Google index URLs with session IDs? How many links to your Web site are needed to get indexed? Note: The introduction is in French, but the interview is in English, just scroll down.
http://chat.abondance.com/google.html

January 2002 Google's CEO How Google earns money. Does advertising on Google affect your ranking?
http://www.pcworld.com/news/article/0,aid,81685,00.asp

May 2001 Google's CTO What gets you banned from Google. Two free ways to get a better ranking on Google.
http://www.ibizinterviews.com/craigs1.htm

November 2000 How is Google organized? What technology is used to operate Google?
http://www.linuxgazette.com/issue59/correa.html

Common Misconceptions about Google

One common mistake made by people is to focus exclusively on Google rankings. The problem with this is that this won't necessarily convert into more money for you. Having a webpage that is easy to navigate and interesting to the user is still very important.

Having good products and services and giving value to the customer is still important. Having good customer service and logistics in your operation will make sure that customers get what they need and keep them coming back to your site.

Increasing traffic to your site will help, but it is important to make sure that other things are in order before you do so. Increasing traffic to a poor website may end up just costing you more money with people emailing you with questions but rarely converting to sales.

Some people are focusing exclusively on Google and forgetting about other things. This is very similar to what happened during the internet bubble 5 years ago. Lots of people during this time were saying things like "It is all about the Internet" and "it's the new economy, stupid".

By focusing and mastering just one tool and thinking that one tool would be the source of all your success is like a carpenter mastering the hammer and then expecting to be successful because of just one tool. The internet and Google are very much the same way.

The internet is just a tool, as were the railroad, the highway, and a nail gun to a carpenter. Tools are just one important part of business. Google is also just a tool. Many other tools are necessary for successful website as well as people.

Another misconception about Google is that there is some sort of special association that companies have with Google that allows them to get at the top of the rankings. Others rumor that advertising on Google helps search engine rankings. This just isn't true. Here is some info taken directly from Google.

Fiction: Advertising on Google affects my rankings in the search results.

Fact: Advertising with Google neither helps (nor hurts!) a site's rankings on Google.

No one can guarantee a #1 ranking on Google.

Beware of SEO's (Search Engine Optimizers) that claim to guarantee rankings, or that claim a "special relationship" with Google, or that claim to have a "priority submit" to Google. There is no priority submit for Google. In fact, the only way to submit a site to Google directly is by using the page at http://www.google.com/addurl.html. You can do this yourself at no cost whatsoever.

You can read more at the links below.

http://www.google.com/webmasters/facts.html
http://www.google.com/webmasters/seo.html

What is a spam webpage?

Spam web pages are sites with little meaningful or relevant content. Below are some more specific examples of spam pages.

Spam webpage's redirect users and have lots of pop-ups. Spam pages use lots of big keywords and few pictures or other more complex elements such as tables, images, etc. Spam pages often use small text, odd colors to hide text such as dark text on black background. Hundreds of pages are created with all links to the main page or other sites. One page may have 20 or more links to the same website. Spam pages will have high keyword density in the body text of a page. Non keywords such as a, an, the will be non-existent in these sites. The same keywords will be used five or more times in a single line of text and Meta tags will be loaded with duplicate keywords.

Bad websites may employ deceptive tricks such as cloaking or serving up different information to web surfers than it does to search engines. Bad websites may employee the use of lots of popup windows or even an endless loop of exit popup windows. Bad websites use non-relevant keywords in pages. A link that says Paris Hilton for instance might go to a site that has nothing to do with Paris Hilton.

Below are some quality guidelines and specific recommendations that Google provides.

Quality Guidelines - Basic principles:

- Make pages for users, not for search engines. Don't deceive your users, or present different content to search engines than you display to users.
- Avoid tricks intended to improve search engine rankings. A good rule of thumb is whether you'd feel comfortable explaining what you've done to a website that competes with you. Another useful test is to ask, "Does this help my users? Would I do this if search engines didn't exist?"
- Don't participate in link schemes designed to increase your site's ranking or PageRank. In particular, avoid links to web spammers or "bad neighborhoods" on the web as your own ranking may be affected adversely by those links.
- Don't use unauthorized computer programs to submit pages, check rankings, etc. Such programs consume computing resources and violate our terms of service. Google does not recommend the use of products such as WebPosition Gold™ that send automatic or programmatic queries to Google.

Quality Guidelines - Specific recommendations:

- Avoid hidden text or hidden links.

- Don't employ cloaking or sneaky redirects.
- Don't send automated queries to Google.
- Don't load pages with irrelevant words.
- Don't create multiple pages, sub domains, or domains with substantially duplicate content.
- Avoid "doorway" pages created just for search engines or other "cookie cutter" approaches such as affiliate programs with little or no original content.

http://www.google.com/webmasters/guidelines.html#quality

Outdated hacks

1. Aggressive keyword repeating
2. One pixel image hyperlink
3. Hidden text
4. Extra long text

1. Aggressive keyword repeating might be putting this into Meta tags, title or body text. An example in body text might be <h1>mp3 download mp3 mp3s mp3 mp3 </h1>
2. One pixel image hyperlinks allow you to hide links you don't want people to see but want search engines to see. This doesn't work much anymore. Use a real text link instead.
3. Hidden text comes in variety of forms. Some people hide it in comment tags in html. Others make text that is very similar to the background color. Keywords are then stuffed into these areas which are barely visible by humans. This isn't as effective as it used to be.
4. Extending meta-description tag, page title, or <h1> tags to be very long isn't going to help anymore. Only the first line or two will be indexed.

Risky Hacks

1. Bait & Switch
2. Cloaking

1. Bait and Switch is simply optimizing a website for a search engine and then redirecting or switching it to another page after it has been indexed by the search engine.

This strategy isn't very sophisticated and is an extremely short term solution. Google indexes very often and will most likely catch the switch shortly after it has been made. Then your site will be penalized after that.

2. Cloaking is a hack that still works today but is very risky. This is another form of fraud to the search engine. What you do is identify the IP addresses and/or bot names for search engines. When search engines go to you site, you forward them to the search engine optimized page and when anyone else goes to that page you show them a different page.

A way of seeing if someone is cloaking or not is to look at the cached page in Google. This can be done by simply clicking on the cached link next to the search result. A cloaked page will show a significantly different site than the site you get when clicking on the Google link.

There are two methods of doing cloaking via user agent detection such as if it says "googlebot" in the log files then it redirects to certain page. The other is IP based detection. Below are some entries for web server log files that show some of the search bots that have visited site. As you can see, you may notice they leave their IP and user agent names behind.

65.213.36.172 - - [26/Jun/2004:17:12:33 -0400] "GET / HTTP/1.0" 302 - "-" "Mozilla/2.0 (compatible; Ask Jeeves/Teoma)" "-"
66.192.90.178 - - [27/Jun/2004:12:40:54 -0400] "GET /robots.txt HTTP/1.0" 404 3417 "-" "Mozilla/5.0 (compatible; Yahoo! Slurp; http://help.yahoo.com/help/us/ysearch/slurp)" "-"
64.67.82.176 - - [26/Jun/2004:12:12:56 -0400] "GET /robots.txt HTTP/1.0" 404 3417 "-" "Googlebot/2.1 (+http://www.googlebot.com/bot.html)" "-"

The IP address will always appear in the logs, but the user agent such as "Googlebot/2.1" can be anything. A typical internet surfer will leave a trail that looks like this:

66.193.6.77 - - [28/Jun/2004:08:43:18 -0400] "GET / HTTP/1.1" 200 3417 "-" "Mozilla/4.0 (compatible; MSIE 6.0; Windows NT 5.1; Q312468)" "-"

In the case above we see that person is using Microsoft Internet Explorer version 6. Google may also have bots that spider websites and don't leave Googlebot/2.1 as the user agent name. Google or other search engines may disguise their bots to show something like MSIE 6.0. Obviously if search engines are disguising themselves cloaking based on user agent becomes useless.

Both methods can be fooled. User agent detection can be easily fooled by Google not announcing itself as googlebot. IP based detection can be fooled if Google changes its IP addresses or adds new ones and you fail to keep up with them.

For this reason, cloaking can be a risky move because it can get your domain banned by Google.

http://www.kloakit.com/dosadonts.html

Getting Banned by Google

Some major abusers of Google have been banned by Google. What does it mean to be banned? Sites that are banned by Google will be entirely removed from Google search engine and will most likely have that domain blocked. Sites that have been banned do not appear even if you do a search for the domain name in Google. Other sites may still have text or links to banned site, but you will not find any links from Google search engine to banned sites. When searching for a domain name of a banned domain in Google, it will return result:

"Sorry, no information is available for the URL"

This does not necessarily mean that your domain is banned permanently. You may be able to simply remove the problem pages such as doorway pages and wait for Google to re-index your domain. Then, your website may come up again in the index. This does not mean that your site hasn't been penalized, though.

If your site was once banned by Google, it may carry a penalty with it and make it difficult to get ranked highly.

Officially, according to Google once banned a re-inclusion request will have to be emailed to Google if you want to have website listed on Google again. And, it is up to them as to whether or not to re-list your site.

Some of these spammers had all or nothing strategies where all sites were linked together to one another. Once banned, all of the spammers other domains were removed as well.

In summary, you want to do the right things and not be deceptive to Google's customers and to Google. Do the right thing and you shouldn't be banned.

The fact is, to be ranked highly on Google you are going to have to work hard whether you cheat or not. You can work hard and be an ethical webmaster or you can work hard and cheat. One is a long term solution while the other is a short term one. If you cheat, you could have your domains pulled from Google and see all your work go down the drain.

Work hard and do things the right way and everyone should be alright.

What is PageRank?

PageRank was developed by Google to help rate sites. Sites are ranked from 0-10 with 10 being the highest.

Here is what Google says about it:

"PageRank relies on the uniquely democratic nature of the web by using its vast link structure as an indicator of an individual page's value. In essence, Google interprets a link from page A to page B as a vote, by page A, for page B. But, Google looks at more than the sheer volume of votes, or links a page receives; it also analyzes the page that casts the vote. Votes cast by pages that are themselves "important" weigh more heavily and help to make other pages "important."

Important, high-quality sites receive a higher PageRank, which Google remembers each time it conducts a search. Of course, important pages mean nothing to you if they don't match your query. So, Google combines PageRank with sophisticated text-matching techniques to find pages that are both important and relevant to your search. Google goes far beyond the number of times a term appears on a page and examines all aspects of the page's content (and the content of the pages linking to it) to determine if it's a good match for your query."

An industry has been cropping up around PR domains. Some people are offering to buy high PR domains from others and are looking for expiring domains with a high PR. The idea is that you buy the high PR domain and then link it to your other sites to improve the PR of your sites.

http://www.google.com/technology/

Page Rank Isn't Everything

The idea that a high PR will always put you on top search results isn't always true. We pulled the top 10 search results from Lycos 50 top sites ending May 1, 2004. http://50.lycos.com/

We will do a quick test to see how relevant PageRank is to top results.

Here is the list:
1. Paris Hilton
2. Clay Aiken
3. Britney Spears
4. KaZaA
5. Weight Watchers

6. Atkins Diet
7. Pam Anderson
8. Dragonball
9. WWE
10. South Beach Diet

I have taken this list and compared Google PageRank for the first 30 results. You will also see ranks 101, 102, 401,402, 701,702. NR means "No Rank." This is caused mostly from string characters in URL from sites such as Amazon.com. The results are on following page.

The results were quite surprising. I expected much higher PR's to be near the top, and much lower ones near the bottom. However, this isn't quite the case; the first and second results have higher ranks, but most of these also happen to be the domain of the company such as Kazaa, Atkins and WWE.

Most of these results had more queries than Google currently indexes. Paris Hilton, for instance had 3,310,000 results. Google will only show up to 835 search result pages for this. I theorized that possibly all of the sites with PR 1 might not be showing up because they are past page 835.

As a result of this, I threw in a specific misspelled keyword "obsure words." This search only had twenty results. I expected the lower PR to be near the bottom, but as you can see this is not so.

The result of these results is quite stunning and seems to point in direction that a very high PR is not extremely important right now to be ranked high by Google. Possibly on future Google updates PR may play a greater role. So, it should still be a priority to focus on keeping PR high, but it is clearly not a major issue right now.

Page Rank of Top 10 Search Words

	Paris Hilton	Clay Aiken	Britney Spears	KaZaA	Weight Watchers	Atkins Diet	Pam Anderson	Dragonball	WWE	South Beach Diet	"obsure
1	5	6	7	7	7	7	5	6	6	NR	
2	5	5	6	7	6	6	5	7	5	NR	
3	5	5	7	6	6	5	4	5	5	NR	▶
4	4	5	5	5	5	4	3	5	NR	6	
5	5	4	5	5	5	6	4	4	5	5	▶
6	4	NR	5	5	5	NR	3	4	6	6	
7	6	4	5	3	5	4	5	4	4	6	
8	4	4	6	5	NR	5	NR	4	NR	5	▶
9	5	4	5	6	NR	5	NR	6	4	4	
10	6	3	9	6	4	6	5	6	5	4	
11	6	4	5	5	6	NR	NR	4	4	4	▶
12	5	6	6	5	5	5	5	4	6	4	
13	4	4	6	6	4	5	5	4	4	5	▶
14	4	3	5	5	5	5	5	4	5	5	
15	6	6	5	5	3	5	4	5	3	6	
16	4	NR	NR	5	4	6	5	4	6	5	
17	4	4	NR	4	4	3	1	4	5	3	▶
18	5	3	6	NR	4	6	6	4	4	5	▶

Google Hacks Exposed

19	5	4	5	4	5	4	4	3	3	6	1
20	5	4	4	NR	6	4	4	4	4	5	5
21	5	1	4	4	NR	5	7	4	4	4	
22	5	2	4	NR	5	5	NR	4	4	5	
23	4	4	5	NR	5	4	1	5	NR	3	
24	3	6	5	3	4	5	4	4	6	7	
25	4	6	4	6	4	4	NR	5	5	4	
26	2	6	4	3	4	5	5	3	6	5	
27	4	5	5	5	NR	4	4	NR	6	4	
28	6	5	5	5	4	NR	4	5	3	4	
29	4	1	4	4	4	NR	4	4	4	4	
30	3	4	NR	4	4	5	3	6	5	4	
101	4	4	4	4	NR	4	3	1	5	NR	
102	5	4	5	4	6	4	NR	4	5	3	
401	1	NR	4	5	3	4	5	3	4	3	
402	NR	2	4	4	NR	4	6	3	4	3	
701	3	2	4	5	3	3	2	3	3	7	
702	4	NR	1	5	NR	4	NR	NR	3	5	

Further Analysis

The above analysis was based on assumption that high PR sites should be near the top of search engine ratings. The info says nothing about PR of sites linking to top search engine ranking sites.

Further research might show that outgoing links from high PR sites are prevalent for sites the in top search results. Unfortunately there is no easy way of compiling this data because of the numerous number of links to the sites and we don't know the weight of each link.

An outgoing link from a site with link text "models" may not play as much of a role as a site that has link text "Paris Hilton" if we are comparing search results for "Paris Hilton."

After looking at that data, it appears that there is very little relationship between high PR and being ranked near top of search results. When it comes to being #1 in search results,

But to simply be on the first search results page this doesn't seem to be the case. On the first page you can see some PR 4 sites and then on the second page you see PR 6's which shows that higher PR sites will not always be ranked higher than lower ones.

In the future we may see more of a relationship between high PR and top ranking. Perhaps in the future, top sites and sites below will be in an order like 8,7,6,6,5,5,4 etc instead of the scattered PR we see right now in the search results.

Doorway Pages

Doorway pages are also sometimes called information pages, hallway pages, or referrer pages. The idea of a doorway page is a simple page optimized for particular keyword or keywords in order to get ranked well by search engines. Doorway pages then usually have links to your flagship site or to another site.

Here are some of rules for doorway pages:

1. Should be optimized for one or two keywords and one engine
2. Should be tailored to each engine's specifications
3. Should never be used for directories like DMOZ
4. Should not be too similar to one another
5. Keywords must be relevant to the website
6. Put doorway pages on an outside domain from the main site
7. Make your doorway pages look good

As a result of abuse by spammers, doorway pages have been given a bad name by search engines.

However, there are some legitimate, non-deceptive uses for doorway pages. If you have a website that is made of mostly images such as an adult site, you may want to have other pages that have text to describe the site so that it gets indexed properly.

Each doorway page should have some keyword links to other internal pages on your site and some keywords in the page.

Each page should be tailored to a specific search engine. In the past, some search engines such as Altavista ranked sites with images in them better than sites without images. Some search engines may like wordier pages than others.

Using a doorway page for directories such as DMOZ is not a wise thing to do. These directories are approved by people. Your goal is probably to get people to your main site. By having an actual human review your site, they can properly link your page in the directory even if you don't have any text on it. Computer based search engines like Google cannot analyze images like humans can and figure out where your site should go. For this reason, when submitting to directories use your main page and not your doorway pages.

Sites that are too similar to one another may be penalized today by Google. So, it is important that you keep the theme of your page not too similar. Using the same doorway page template for all of your doorway pages is probably not the way to go. Expect to have around 10-20 doorway pages per domain but keep them a little different from one another.

Your keywords on your doorway pages must be similar to what you have on your site. Don't add irrelevant keywords to the page with the hope that you will get more traffic from more places. The greater the number of less relevant keywords you add, the more your pages start looking like spam and the greater the chance you have of getting your pages removed from the index or penalized.

If you own the main website that you are trying to point your doorway pages to, you probably don't want to create doorway pages on your main website for security reasons.

If your main webpage gets banned this is probably worst than if you get banned on one of your doorway page domains. You can always produce new domains and doorway page sites, but if your main website gets tarnished this is much more difficult to fix.

Your doorway pages should also look nice. They should look like regular websites with images and readable text. As web surfers grow more sophisticated, they are learning how to spot doorway pages by their unreadable text and lack of pictures.

Doorway pages have given many people a bad experience. Endless popup windows, software install popup boxes and other nuisances. Once someone notices what doorway page search descriptions look like, many of them may not click the links.

If you can make your doorway pages look nice, you will be able to get newbies as well as sophisticated surfers to click on your links in Google as well as the links on your doorway pages.

For more sophisticated doorway pages, look at the Army of Sites section in this book.

Good vs. Bad Doorway Pages

The idea that all doorway pages are bad just isn't true even though you may hear many people say this on forums and websites.

The fact is a good doorway page may look very much like a regular page. A good doorway page will be readable, have images and look nice.

The difference between a doorway page and regular webpage is that a doorway page's intention is to get ranked highly by search engines by being very search engine readable.

A regular website is based more around the end user with less emphasis on search engine visibility.

The thing that has given doorway pages a bad name is because many doorway pages have been used exclusively for one purpose, search engine visibility without including anything such as being based around the user experience.

This lack of compromise has led to doorway pages that are ugly and loaded with random keywords with little else. This provides little interest to people browsing the site and isn't very valuable to people.

A new trend with doorway pages should be a balance between search engine visibility and usability for people. This is something that will help to give doorway pages a better name.

When done correctly, you are doing a good thing for your web surfers as well as the search engines themselves. Without providing search engine friendly web pages, you are keeping people and search engines of your valuable material. Good doorway pages make your valuable information available to search engines and people. This is what both people and Google want.

Highly publicized hacks

Below are some search terms of some highly publicized hacks. These work on both Yahoo and Google search engines. Near the top of the search results you may notice some non-relevant web pages. Here are the search terms below:

1: weapons of mass destruction
2: waffles
3. miserable failure

1. weapons of mass destruction - At top of the search results is a page that looks like a dead link page that says "Cannot find Weapons of Mass Destruction." The URL is www.coxar.pwp.blueyonder.co.uk

Web | Images | Groups | News | Froogle[New!] | **more »**

weapons of mass destruction | Search | Adv
Pref

"**of**" is a very common word and was not included in your searc

---

Web

Results **1 - 10** of about **2,140,0**

Cannot find **Weapons** of **Mass Destruction**

These **Weapons** of **Mass Destruction** cannot be displayed. The **weapons** you are looking
for are currently unavailable. The country might ...
www.coxar.pwp.blueyonder.co.uk/ - 5k - May 3, 2004 - Cached - Similar pages

CNS - **Weapons** of **Mass Destruction** in the Middle East

Weapons of **Mass Destruction** in the Middle East. Overviews on Nuclear, Biological, and
Chemical (NBC) **Weapons**. ...
cns.miis.edu/research/wmdme/ - 10k - Cached - Similar pages

FindLaw's Writ - Dean: Missing **Weapons** Of **Mass Destruction**

... --- Missing **Weapons** Of **Mass Destruction**: Is Lying About The Reason For War An
Impeachable Offense? By JOHN W. DEAN ---- Friday, Jun. 06, 2003. ...
writ.news.findlaw.com/dean/20030606.html - 51k - May 3, 2004 - Cached - Similar pages

[PDF] CWMD
File Format: PDF/Adobe Acrobat - View as HTML
... N ATIONAL S TRATEGY TO C OMBAT W EAPONS OF M ASS D ESTRUCTION 1
National Strategy to Combat **Weapons** of **Mass Destruction** "The gravest danger our
Nation faces ...
www.whitehouse.gov/news/releases/ 2002/12/WMDStrategy.pdf - Similar pages

Google Hacks Exposed

ⓘ These Weapons of Mass Destruction cannot be displayed

The weapons you are looking for are currently unavailable. The country might be experiencing technical difficulties, or you may need to adjust your weapons inspectors mandate.

Please try the following:

- Click the 🗘 Regime change button, or try again later.
- If you are George Bush and typed the country's name in the address bar, make sure that it is spelled correctly. (IRAQ).
- To check your weapons inspector settings, click the **UN** menu, and then click **Weapons Inspector Options**. On the **Security Council** tab, click **Consensus**. The settings should match those provided by your government or NATO.
- If the Security Council has enabled it, The United States of America can examine your country and automatically discover Weapons of Mass Destruction.
  If you would like to use the CIA to try and discover them, click 🔍 Detect weapons
- Some countries require 128 thousand troops to liberate them. Click the **Panic** menu and then click **About US foreign policy** to determine what regime they will install.
- If you are an Old European Country trying to protect your interests, make sure your options are left wide open as long as possible. Click the **Tools** menu, and then click on **League of Nations**. On the Advanced tab, scroll to the Head in the Sand section and check settings for your exports to Iraq.
- Click the 💣 Bomb button if you are Donald Rumsfeld.

Cannot find weapons or CIA Error
Iraqi Explorer
Bush went to Iraq to look for Weapons of Mass Destruction and all he found was this lousy T-shirt.

The page has some keywords on it that say weapons, but the page doesn't have very many keywords or links. What is very interesting is the # of links to it. When we do Google search for:

link:www.coxar.pwp.blueyonder.co.uk/ we see that there are 648 sites are linking to it. When looking at these sites we see that most have links on their pages that read "weapons of mass destruction" or some similar variant of it.

http://www.usatoday.com/tech/news/2004-04-11-kerry-waffles_x.htm

2: waffles. Recently a similar trick was done with John Kerry. Within 8 days, johnkerry.com was listed second with 703,000 results on Yahoo for the word "waffles" It took a little while longer for Google to catch it, but when it is also has johnkerry.com as #1 for waffles.

Web   Images   Groups   News   Froogle^{New!}   **more »**

waffles   [Search]   Advan
                                                        Prefer

Web   Results **1 - 10**

:: John Kerry for President - Welcome to JohnKerry.com! ::
GET KERRY EMAIL. ...
www.johnkerry.com/ - 49k - May 4, 2004 - Cached - Similar pages

Recipes, **Waffles** - Bed & Breakfast Inns ONLINE
Bed & Breakfast Inns ONLINE, **Waffles** Recipes We've got **Waffles!** ... Delicious? Yes:
every one is innkeeper tested, and guest approved! **Waffles** Recipes. ...
www.bbonline.com/recipe/**waffles**.html - 10k - Cached - Similar pages

Western **Waffles** Flash HomePage
extranet, Western **Waffles** produces over 2 million **waffles** per day; translating into 25
waffles per second. site design © 2003 bSmart ...
www.western**waffles**.com/ - 6k - May 3, 2004 - Cached - Similar pages

BABEL
Belgian **Waffles** In a way, you could say that there are no "Belgian" **waffles**, but there is
rather a whole bunch of varieties. ... Flemish **Waffles**. ...
www.geocities.com/SoHo/2830/bbwaff.html - 10k - Cached - Similar pages

John Kerry's **Waffles** - If you don't like the Democratic nominee's ...
politics, Who's winning, who's losing, and why. John Kerry's **Waffles** If you don't like the
Democratic nominee's views, just wait a week. ...
slate.msn.com/id/2096540/ - 39k - May 3, 2004 - Cached - Similar pages

hotwaffles.com
hotwaffles.com;http://s93361401.onlinehome.us;.
www.hot**waffles**.com/ - 1k - Cached - Similar pages

waffles on web
waffles on web.
www.**waffles**.jp/ - 1k - Cached - Similar pages

Lee Stranahan - Roscoe's Chicken 'n **Waffles** Page
THE BEST **WAFFLES** IN THE WORLD!!!! Okay, a lot of people find the ideas of Chicken
and **Waffles** on the same plate odd. I used to find it odd, but I like odd. ...

Web-savvy jokers call this scheme to push Internet users to a
specific Web site "Google bombing." It takes a coordinated effort
by many Web sites and blogs to accomplish this. A blog is an
online journal or diary that is available over the internet and

usually updated daily. Blogs are often highly personal and cover a variety of topics.

Miserable failure. This site lists the Whitehouse website at top of search results for "Miserable failure" and has a nice photo of George Bush when you enter the webpage. Also listed below the Whitehouse page is a biography of Jimmy Carter and Michael Moore's site. These sites also appear under "failure" as well. **(approx 2,250 sites are linking to the George Bush bio page)**

miserable failure   [Search]   Advanced S
                                               Preferences

Web   Results **1 - 10** of ab

Biography of President George W. Bush
Home > President > Biography President George W. Bush En Español. George W. Bush
is the 43rd President of the United States. He ...
www.whitehouse.gov/president/gwbbio.html - 29k - Cached - Similar pages

Biography of Jimmy Carter
Home > History & Tours > Past Presidents > Jimmy Carter. Jimmy Carter. Jimmy Carter
aspired to make Government "competent and compassionate ...
www.whitehouse.gov/history/presidents/jc39.html - 35k - Cached - Similar pages

Michael Moore.com
Click Here To Continue To MichaelMoore.Com. Click Here To Continue To
MichaelMoore.Com.
www.michaelmoore.com/ - 5k - Cached - Similar pages

BBC NEWS | Americas | 'Miserable failure' links to Bush
'Miserable failure' links to Bush. ... Prank website. Newsday newspaper says as few as
32 web pages with the words "miserable failure" link to the Bush biography. ...
news.bbc.co.uk/2/hi/americas/3298443.stm - 31k - Cached - Similar pages

Atlantic Unbound | Politics & Prose | 2003.09.24
... Atlantic Unbound | September 24, 2003 Politics & Prose | by Jack Beatty "A Miserable
Failure" Will Bush be re-elected? Only if voters ...
www.theatlantic.com/unbound/polipro/pp2003-09-24.htm - 21k - Cached - Similar pages

Senator Hillary Rodham Clinton: Online Office Welcome Page
Dear Friend,. Thank you for visiting my on-line office! I appreciate your interest in the issues
before the United States Senate. ...
clinton.senate.gov/ - 10k - Cached - Similar pages

Google's (and Inktomi's) Miserable Failure
A search for miserable failure on Google brings up the official George W. Bush biography
from the US White House web site. Dismissed ...
searchenginewatch.com/sereport/article.php/3296101 - 48k - Cached - Similar pages

The thing about Google bombing is it may be deceptive to the
search engine user. For example, nowhere on the George Bush
Whitehouse page do you see any keywords about failure.
Instead, of listing all of the sites that say miserable failure on
them, Google is trusting that the George Bush site should be
listed under miserable failure and is putting George Bush at the
top of list for "failure." And, someone else that truly has a site
about failure is getting pushed down the ranks by this trick.

Google is taking the votes of many sites to be more important than one single vote from the actual site that everyone is referring to. And, Google seems to accept their votes without checking out the sources. Google could index the George Bush site and look for words "miserable failure" or something similar to it but it doesn't seem to do this. If there is no match or similarity between keywords on the George bush site and referring sites then the George Bush site should not be on top of list for miserable failure.

However, Google does not do this. It simply takes the votes of the linking sites as being reliable. This is similar to a major newspaper posting a story without ever checking the source simply because it has numerous sources that orally state a similar story.

Google has officially stated that it doesn't view "Google bombing" as much of a threat because it isn't very widespread and it usually features obscure keywords that aren't very popular. This statement really says nothing about it being ok to do. Google is just stating that it isn't widely abused yet. Just wait until it is and their opinion should change.

Words like "failure" and "waffles" are not very popular keywords. The question is would it work for a very popular keyword like "sex" or "mp3."?

http://www.microcontentnews.com/articles/googleblogs.htm

Some have taken this into their own hands and have purchased hundreds of domain names and setup numerous websites that all point to the same URL. These doorway pages usually have the same layout and are pretty much unreadable by most users with random text scattered throughout the pages.

Google has caught on to this and since about Jan 04, has stopped lots of these spammers. Now, Google seems to be comparing the directory structure of pages and this spamming technique will not work as well anymore.

Google Hacks Exposed

This type of hack can be quite challenging. Besides acquiring many domains and web hosts, pages have to be made for each of them. Most of the people that have done this use some type of script that provides the automatic creation of pages.

Then, there is typically 10 links or so on each page that point either to other pages on that domain or to other domain web pages. All pages look almost identical with lots of keywords and keyword links.

Some link all their sites together while others focus on using all the domains to promote one site by linking just to that one.

Google has been cracking down on this type of spamming since the last "Florida" update. As the search engine algorithms get more advanced, it will become more difficult to do this type of spamming.

The relationships between all of the domains will start becoming known as search engine technology advances. The file size of all the pages will be about the same. The table structure for each site looks the same as well as # of links and pictures. The more similar the sites look, the more it looks like spamming to Google.

In the future, it might go further than that to look at name server (DNS Server) info for each domain, and registry info for domains. When looking at a variety of factors, these sites will start looking like they are all part of one another instead of appearing as though they were all independent domains.

Folder Names

Your website will be stored in a folder in usually a Linux or Windows Server. All subfolders within this folder can be named in a specific way so that folder name acts as keyword. Instead of folder /book/ for instance, you can name it something more specific like /computer-book/.

This may not affect much for most searches, but when someone starts doing a deeper search, it will become more important.

Page Name

Besides folder names, page names are also important. Your main page in your web folder is usually index.htm or index.html. For Windows servers it is something like default.htm. Since these are defaults, a user typing in http://www.yourdomain.com/ will default to these files if they are in the directory.

The default pages are transparent to the web surfer. Whenever someone types in a domain.com into the URL, the user may only see domain.com in the URL window but what they are actually seeing is http://domain.com/index.htm or whatever the default page is called.

These files can be changed to point to whatever name you want. In web server software Apache, here is typical configuration for this:

DirectoryIndex index.shtml index.html index.html.var

You can change this to:

DirectoryIndex index.shtml index.html index.html.var keyword.html

As you see, keyword.html is added and you could call the keyword whatever you want such as googlehacks.html. Now, whenever someone types in your domain, it will default to keyword.html if the other files in front of it are not present. The web server software will default to the first files you have in file so index.shtml in our example, has priority over the others. All of this can be changed to whatever order you want.

This example isn't probably going to help you with search engines because it becomes hidden to search engine if only domain is typed into browser. This is just a technical trick that may be helpful to you. http://yourdomain.com could be defaulting to any page you specify and search engines have no idea what it is.

Your non-default page names can actually be seen by users and search engines. Instead of leaving basic page names for your pages such as page1.html or page2.html change these to keyword names such as keyword1.htm, my-favorite-keywords.htm, etc. This will make them more important to search engines.

When creating links on your pages, you may want to point to absolute paths instead of relative paths. If you are creating a link on a webpage, you could simply add a link like:

<a href="/chocolate-candy.html">Chocolate Candy</a>

However, it might be more useful to include absolute path:

<a href=http://surplus-candy.bobs-chocolates.com/chocolate-candy.html>Chocolate Candy</a>

The second example contains more keywords than the first example and may help your search engine ratings for these keywords.

When requesting others to link to your site, you may also request that they link to your absolute path (domain plus the page name) instead of just the domain name. So, like the second example above, you would ask them to link to the hyperlink similar to second style as opposed to just linking to the domain name.

Make sure that your page names do not contain strings such as index.php?=. These odd characters aren't indexed as well with Google.

In the section below, you will find out more about page name optimization.

Domain Name

Besides page optimization, URL optimization also plays a role in search engine results. Owning the domain for a keyword is still the best thing, but if you don't own a domain for the entire keyword, you can always purchase similar domains with a keyword in it or modify you current domain. A search for "mp3" in Google returns mp3.com domain as the top ranking site.

 Web　Images　Groups　News　Froogle^{New!}　**more »**

mp3　　　　　　　　　　　　　　　　　　Search　Advanced
　　　　　　　　　　　　　　　　　　　　　　　　Preferenc

Web

 News results for **mp3** - View all the latest headlines
Ashampoo **MP3** Audio Center 1.5 - VNUNet.com - 9 hours ago
Cnet to reintroduce **MP3**.com - San Francisco Chronicle - May 3, 2004

MP3.com
MP3.com. Hours away from launch! Working night ... soon. If you love digital music, you'll
be glad to see the new **MP3**.com. What We'll Be. We ...
www.**mp3**.com/ - 5k - May 3, 2004 - Cached - Similar pages

WINAMP.COM | What the hell is NtUserCallHwndLock?
NULLSOFT WINAMP, MY PROFILE LOG IN SUPPORT, Home, Player, Skins, Plug-ins,
Music, Video/Films, Games, Community, Development, Welcome News About Us Team
Nullsoft, ...
www.winamp.com/ - 31k - May 3, 2004 - Cached - Similar pages

WINAMP.COM | Player
... your CDs at speeds up to 48x, 9 times the speed of Winamp 5! (Actual speeds may
differ, depending on your computer's specifications.) **MP3** Encoding — With ...
www.winamp.com/download/ - 15k - Cached - Similar pages
[More results from www.winamp.com]

Lycos Music | Downloads
Lycos Music Downloads: search for **MP3** files, download the Lycos Music Player powered
by Sonique, read an **MP3** how-to guide or find and host **MP3** files from ...
music.lycos.com/downloads/ - 41k - May 3, 2004 - Cached - Similar pages

mp3.box :: mp3 and music related news and tools
Software, encoders, • Alive WMA **MP3** Recorder Alive WMA **MP3** Recorder records any
audio source from your computer into **MP3**, WAV, WMA, OGG, and VOX ... ...
mp3.box.sk/ - 38k - May 3, 2004 - Cached - Similar pages

Napster.com
Get instant access to more tracks for less cash with Napster Premium. Legally listen to
and download over 500,000 tracks for less than 10 bucks per month. ...
www.napster.com/ - 15k - May 3, 2004 - Cached - Similar pages

On the same page we also see some very popular sites as well
as: http://mp3.box.sk/, and on second page we see variations of

Web

Jumbo: Free & Shareware **MP3** files, Games, Screen Savers & Computer ...
Jumbo is the source for free **MP3** files, games, desktop themes,
screen savers and the latest computer software. ...
www.jumbo.com/ - 47k - May 3, 2004 - Cached - Similar pages

??????——chinamp3.com
The summary for this Chinese (Simplified) page contains characters that cannot be correctly disp.
www.china**mp3**.com/ - 38k - May 3, 2004 - Cached - Similar pages

mp3.de - Musik im Internet - [Translate this page]
mp3.de - Musik im Internet. Freier **MP3**-Download aus etwa 100 Genres.
Große Community sowie Charts, Infos und News zu **MP3**. mp3.de, ...
www.**mp3**.de/ - 80k - May 3, 2004 - Cached - Similar pages

Libero - [Translate this page]
Home, Accesso Internet, Mail, Ricerca, Community, News, Canali, Shopping,
Broadband, i-mode TM. Web, Immagini, Video, Gruppi, **Mp3**, Directory,
con ...
www.libero.it/ - 61k - May 3, 2004 - Cached - Similar pages

eMusic | **MP3** subscription service. Free MP3s.
MP3 subscription service. Over 200000 MP3s for download. Free MP3s. ... Howlin'
Wolf, Stop Using Me, KEY» download full **MP3**: | hear **MP3** sample: ...
www.emusic.com/ - 51k - May 3, 2004 - Cached - Similar pages

Real.com - Accessories
By converting cumbersome WAVs into compact, high-quality **MP3** files at lightning
speed, the encoder makes it easy to build a library of digital music. ...
www.xingtech.com/ - 30k - May 3, 2004 - Cached - Similar pages

LAME Ain't an **MP3** Encoder
The LAME Project. LAME is an LGPL **MP3** encoder. The Open source development ... Technical
Details (**MP3** Encoding and LAME). Join the **mp3** encoding ...
www.**mp3**dev.org/**mp3**/ - 4k - Cached - Similar pages

this: **mp3**.baidu.com/,   www.china**mp3**.com/   www.**mp3**.de/
www.**mp3**dev.org/**mp3**/ www.**mp3**-2000.com/

The domains you own you can make sub domains such as:
mp3.yourdomain.com or keyword.yourdomain.com. This will

most likely improve rankings for "mp3" keyword. This can be done by modifying your DNS settings and web server software settings. Ask your webmaster or web administrator and most should be able to do this for you.

Besides your domain, you may also do this with your page names. So, for your index page, you could make this mp3.htm and you could make mp3.htm default page for that site. On your other pages on site, you could name them freemp3s.htm, kazaamp3.htm, and so on.

Google gives priority to top level domains, so it will usually put sites like mp3.com above, mp3.com/mp3page2.htm or mp3.com/directory1/mp3/index.htm.

So, you will want to keep your pages closer to the domain and not too far away or buried in directories. A far away link structure would be something like yourdomain.com/1/key/3/direct/key/mp3.htm. Notice all of the directories in front of mp3.htm. This could possibly make mp3.htm less important to Google because it is so far away from domain. If this is not an issue now, it will most likely be in the future as a result of spammers so you might want to prepare for this.

Google is very sophisticated in the different ways you can search. Your users are probably not, however. A search for free mp3 file download in Google is probably more common than a specific search with quotations "free mp3 file download". The first method looks for words scattered across the page: the second looks for all of the words together.

Web

MP3.com
... upload music. CNET **Download**.com Music Has Launched. **Download** thousands of
free MP3s from independent artists at CNET **Download**.com's new music section.
Newsletter. ...
www.**mp3**.com/ - 5k - May 3, 2004 - Cached - Similar pages

free mp3 download from MP3DD
MP3DD: **mp3** search engine for finding **free mp3** direct **downloads**. The ... Powerful **mp3**
search engine for finding **free mp3 downloads**. The ...
www.**mp3**dd.net/ - 18k - May 3, 2004 - Cached - Similar pages

eMusic | MP3 subscription service. Free MP3s.
MP3 subscription service. Over 200000 **MP3s** for **download**. **Free MP3s**. Virus **free**, high
quality, legal **MP3s**. Home, ...
www.emusic.com/ - 51k - May 3, 2004 - Cached - Similar pages

Ampcast.com: free mp3 downloads, music and CDs of musical artists
Your source for **free** music and **MP3s** to play or **download**, artist CDs, **free MP3**
software, **MP3** news, **MP3** product reviews, **free** personal account for CDs and **MP3s** ...
www.ampcast.com/ - 55k - May 3, 2004 - Cached - Similar pages

YourMP3.Net: Free MP3 Download Archive. Find Your Favorite MP3s !
We Offer 150000 mp3 Downloads from an Archive to browse from. Download songs,
download full albums, download MTV charts, lyrics. Updated Daily.
www.your**mp3**.net/ - 3k - Cached - Similar pages

Mp3Raid.com ||| Free Mp3 Downloads | Mp3 Search | Charts | Full ...
... **Download free MP3** DANCER now Want a Disco Dancer on your desktop? **download**
free MP3 DANCER now **MP3** SEARCH ENGINE One of the best **mp3** search engines on
the net. ...
www.**mp3**raid.com/ - 20k - May 3, 2004 - Cached - Similar pages

Free mp3 music player downloads, countdown songs charts, freeware ...
... DOWNLOAD FREE MP3 SONGS - FULL ALBUMS AZ - 100% **FREE** FAST DIRECT
MP3 SERVER - DOWNLOAD / LISTEN / SEARCH / CDs, 54, 209. ... **FREE MP3**
ALBUMS - **Free MP3 Downloads**. ...
www.**free-mp3**-music-player-**downloads**.com/ - 29k - May 3, 2004 - Cached -
Similar pages

The second method returns some sites that are much different from the first method. Notice that in the second example that free "mp3 download" words are always directly next to one another in the search results. The first result allows other words to get in between the search words in the search such as "free mp3 music player downloads."

Web

free mp3 download from MP3DD

MP3DD: Powerful mp3 search engine for finding free mp3 downloads limp bizkit -
backstreet boys - metallica - r&b - tupac - offspring - britney spears - sublime. ...
www.mp3dd.net/ - 18k - May 3, 2004 - Cached - Similar pages

YourMP3.Net: **Free MP3 Download** Archive. Find Your Favorite MP3s !

We Offer 150000 mp3 Downloads from an Archive to browse from. Download songs,
download full albums, download MTV charts, lyrics. Updated Daily.
www.yourmp3.net/ - 3k - Cached - Similar pages

MP3.com

MP3.com. Hours away from launch! Working night and day, our lean mean team is
tightening the drums, tuning the strings, and banging ...
www.mp3.com/ - 5k - May 3, 2004 - Cached - Similar pages

Free MP3 Music and **Free mp3 download**

Free Mp3 Music **Free Mp3 Download** Free Mp3 Radio Free Mp3 search engine Free
Music download. - Your Final Mp3 Destination Search: ...
www.mp3daze.com/ - 31k - Cached - Similar pages

free trance mp3 download

100% **free mp3 download** - huge mp3 archive - full mp3 albums and singles A/Z - fast
mp3 server - download / listen / charts / search / CDs. ...
www.hard-trance.com/ - 2k - May 3, 2004 - Cached - Similar pages

Free MP3 Downloads - MP3hi-fi.com

Main. Free MP3 Downloads. Full Mp3 Albums. Fragrances. Shoes Online. Bookmark Us.
MP3 Charts. Europe TOP 100. World TOP 40. UK TOP 50. MTV TOP 20. Australia TOP
30. ...
www.mp3hi-fi.com/ - 19k - May 3, 2004 - Cached - Similar pages

BeSonic - the **free MP3 download** portal

Industrial Dance. So, we meet again! (The Samurai Part 2) GinNger SparklezZz The
intriguing sounds and beats that are born within ...
www.besonic.com/BeSonic/Home/ 0,4601,g0r0l0t0o0i0,FF.html - 52k - May 3, 2004 -
Cached - Similar pages

Owning .com and .net domains are still the best.

Due to spammers abusing Google, it appears that .us, .info and the other low priced domains are being penalized. If you do some searches now on Google, you will probably see very few .us or .info near the top of the search results. This may just be that Google is now effective at banning spammers who mostly used .us and .info domains, but it may also be that Google is penalizing .us and .info domains.

Some individual spammers purchased thousands of these low priced domains and made thousands of doorway pages with very little information on each page. This may be the cause of the decline on .us, .info, and other new domains in search engine results.

Another thing that seems to have happened as result of this is that dashes (-) in domain names doesn't seem to be as common anymore in search results. Before Google's update in November, in searches there were lots of domains like free-mp3-download-movies-warez.com in search results. Now you rarely see more than one or two dashes in the top search results.

This certainly makes sense when you look at the ideas for the ideal search engine. The ideal search engine will not make webmasters do anything too sophisticated to get ranked high. Most people do not want a company website domain with lots of dashes in it. They will purchase domains with probably no more than two dashes in it. Once you start getting more than that, the person is probably thinking too much about search engines, and that is not good for the ideal search engine concept. If the user is doing too much thinking about things like that, Google must think that it is spam.

Misspellings & Mistyping

Many people misspell words, so don't be afraid to have some of the names or keywords in a page misspelled. You probably don't want to misspell keywords in your main page, but on some of your leader pages you may want some of these.

People may also mistype keywords. People with large fingers or when tired may accidentally hit the wrong keys. One of the ways people mistype is by not lining up fingers on the correct keys. On the left hand, the natural typing arrangement is a,s,d,f and for right hand it is j,k,l,;. The person may accidentally move the left hand one key to right to be on, s,d,f,g and for right hand, they may move to left to be on keys h,j,k,l. So, you may want to try typing in your keywords with these keys. Most likely a person will catch the mistake after a few keystrokes so don't expect this trick to work on long keywords.

Another way people mistype is by being fatigued or typing too fast. Try typing in your keywords real fast late at night when you are tired and see what type of variations you get on your keywords. Write down these variations and try to use them in some of your pages.

Besides these types of misspellings there are also language related misspellings. People that speak English as a second language for instance may misspell certain words. Asian people may for instance make plural words singular by leaving "s" off from most plural words. Microsoft Windows XP may become "Window XP" instead of "Windows XP."

Other words like "organization" may be misspelled as "organisation." These are just a couple of examples that you may want to think about.

Some have taken this issue even further and purchased misspelled domains for popular websites.

Abbreviations

Besides misspellings words are often abbreviated. Search engine optimization abbreviated becomes SEO. Not all words are commonly abbreviated by people, but over time it may happen. Here are some examples:

Electronic mail became email. World Wide Web became www. American Online became AOL. Kentucky Fried Chicken became

KFC. International Business Machines became IBM. General Electric became GE. General Motors became GM. Instant Messenger is sometimes referred to as IM.

When looking for keywords to use for your business or website, think of some abbreviations that you can use. These things should help your ranking.

Plural Searches

A search for mp3 player and mp3 players will not return the same results. What is the difference? One is plural and one is not.

If you had "mp3 players" in your page title, and wanted to get more users typing in "mp3 player", you could drop the "s" in "players" for your page title and see your ranking jump up for this. Your rating for "mp3 players" would however go down.

Web   Images   Groups   News   Froogle   **more »**

| mp3 player | [Search] | Advanced Searcl |
| | | Preferences |

Veb

---

p3 player
op.NPR.org   Geek it up at the NPR Store. Purchases support NPR programming.

et a Free MP3 Player.
ww.napster.com   With 1-year subscription to Napster Legal. Safe. Easy. Get it Now!

---

oduct search results for **mp3 player**

256MB JetFlash **MP3 Player**/Recorder (P/N TS256MJFLASHM) - $96.98 - We Love Macs!
Creative Labs Nomad MuVo NX128MB **MP3 Player** - $99.95 - Discovery Store
Creative Rhomba 256MB Grey **MP3 Player** - $169.99 - Outpost.com

INAMP.COM | I have a broad personal choice to be me and to have ...
ILLSOFT WINAMP, MY PROFILE LOG IN SUPPORT, Home, **Player**, Skins, Plug-ins,
ısic, Video/Films, Games, Community, Development, Welcome News About Us Team
·llsoft, **...**
/w.winamp.com/ - 31k - Jun 23, 2004 - Cached - Similar pages

> **WINAMP.COM | Player**
> ... When all your songs are encoded in **MP3**, it provides you the freedom to play them in all
> **MP3** capable hardware and software media **players**. ...
> www.winamp.com/download/ - 15k - Cached - Similar pages
> [More results from www.winamp.com]

P3.com - the source for digital music!
Digital Music Services; Portable **Players**; Software; Tools & Tips. Newsletter. Newsletter
ın up Sign up for the **MP3**.com newsletter and get the latest music buzz ...
/w.**mp3**.com/ - 26k - Jun 23, 2004 - Cached - Similar pages

usicmatch Jukebox Digital Audio Software:
Musicmatch Jukebox Winner of PC Magazine Editors' Choice Award for Best Music
ayer. - five times in a row! Rip, burn, play and manage your CDs, **MP3s** and more ...
ww.musicmatch.com/ - 14k - Cached - Similar pages

onique Web v3.0
Get Sonique2 Info privacy statement. WHAT IS SONIQUE? SONIQUE 1.96 · The Ultimate
ıdio **Player** · Sonique is the Web's hottest media and **MP3 player**. ...
nique.lycos.com/ - 26k - Jun 23, 2004 - Cached - Similar pages

---

Google Hacks Exposed   49

Differences in search results

mp3 player	mp3 players
1. winamp.com	1. mp3.com
2. winamp.com	2. winamp.com
3. mp3.com	3. winamp.com
4. musicmatch.com	4. musicmatch.com
5. sonique.lycos.com	5. apple.com

Web

eals on **MP3 Players**
uy.com   Nomad, Creative Labs, Joybee and More. Free Shipping Available. affi

ews results for **mp3 players** - View today's top stories
Toshiba unveils mini fuel cell for **MP3 players** - VNUNet.com - 9 hours ago

P3.com - the source for digital music!
Digital Music Services; Portable **Players**; Software; Tools & Tips. Newsletter. Newsletter
gn up Sign up for the **MP3**.com newsletter and get the latest music buzz ...
ww.**mp3**.com/ - 26k - Jun 23, 2004 - Cached - Similar pages

fINAMP.COM | I have a broad personal choice to be me and to have ...
JLLSOFT WINAMP, MY PROFILE LOG IN SUPPORT, Home, **Player**, Skins, Plug-ins,
usic, Video/Films, Games, Community, Development, Welcome News About Us Team
Jllsoft, ...
ww.winamp.com/ - 31k - Jun 23, 2004 - Cached - Similar pages

WINAMP.COM | **Player**
... When all your songs are encoded in **MP3**, it provides you the freedom to play them in all
MP3 capable hardware and software media **players**. ...
www.winamp.com/player/ - 15k - Jun 23, 2004 - Cached - Similar pages

lusicmatch Jukebox Digital Audio Software:
ownload Musicmatch Jukebox Winner of PC Magazine Editors' Choice Award for Best Music
layer. - five times in a row! Rip, burn, play ...
ww.musicmatch.com/ - 14k - Cached - Similar pages

pple - iPod
, music **player** that supports the AAC format used by the iTunes Music Store for Mac and
/indows. AAC features CD-quality audio in smaller file sizes than **MP3**, so ...
ww.apple.com/ipod/ - 25k - Cached - Similar pages

onique Web v3.0
, Get Sonique2 Info privacy statement. WHAT IS SONIQUE? SONIQUE 1.96 · The Ultimate
udio **Player** · Sonique is the Web's hottest media and **MP3 player**. ...
onique.lycos.com/ - 26k - Jun 23, 2004 - Cached - Similar pages

As you can see, the search results are different. For the particular example used, some of the top sites still remain on the first page in either search, but the rankings are different. This is just one example; in other examples the sites may be totally dropped from first two search result pages just by adding or subtracting an "s" from your page title.

So, you may want to make some extra pages for singular or plural searches. If you duplicate a page, you may want to modify it so that it doesn't look too similar to your other page. If they are too similar, it might be pegged as doorway page and be penalized.

Page Title

The page title is a very important part of optimization strategy. The title should be brief with some keywords in it. Here is a search for computer systems in Google. Notice the highlighted page titles matching the keywords.

Google

computer systems   [Search]   Advanced Search / Preferences

Web

Sony Computers- Save $250
www.SonyStyle.com   On VAIO Desktop & Display Packages Buy Now - The Official Sony Store!

Gateway - Official Site
www.gateway.com   Desktops Starting at $400 & Laptops from $900. Free shipping offer!

News results for **computer systems** - View all the latest headlines
Microsoft CEO outlines IT **systems** software effort - Forbes - Apr 28, 2004

The Public-Access **Computer Systems** Review
... A Brief History of the Journal. The Public-Access **Computer Systems** Review (PACS Review)
was an electronic journal about end-user **computer systems** in libraries. ...
info.lib.uh.edu/pr/pacsrev.html - 19k - Apr 29, 2004 - Cached - Similar pages

Mercury **Computer Systems** Inc.
Mercury **Computer Systems**, Inc. delivers embedded, real-time multicomputers
that transform large streams of sensor data to information ...
www.mc.com/ - 48k - Apr 29, 2004 - Cached - Similar pages - Stock quotes: MRCY

Intergraph Solutions
AM/FM/GIS solutions for the utilities industry, including communications, gas, pipeline, electric,...
www.intergraph.com/ - 2k - Cached - Similar pages - Stock quotes: INGR

Welcome to SGI
... Development. **Systems** Engineering Professional Services Managed Services
Support Services Customer Education Online Support. Games ...
www.sgi.com/ - 25k - Apr 29, 2004 - Cached - Similar pages - Stock quotes: SGI

Elitegroup **Computer Systems** Co., Ltd. -- USA
... Home | Terms of Use | Privacy Policy | Contact | ©2004 Elitegroup **Computer**
Systems. All Rights Reserved. All trademarks are properties ...
www.ecsusa.com/ - 15k - Cached - Similar pages

TOCS
... Browse ACM Transactions on **Computer Systems** (TOCS): ... ACM Transactions on **Computer Systems**
(TOCS) publishes the newest findings of the computing research field. ...

The title should not be too long because Google isn't going to pull keywords past the first eight words or so. And, as you can see the page title shows up in the search results as the description for your website. Metatag descriptions will not always get indexed by Google, so this will be your only real website description unless you put a line of text at the top of the website.

So, it is important that your title readable by users as well as having some keywords in it.

Another thing that is worth mentioning is that you will probably want to have your domain name or name of your business in the page title of the main page. When trying to optimize the page title, you may notice that if you get rid of your website name on the main page title, that when you do a search for your website name in Google, your main site might not come up first, but your secondary pages will come up first because they have your business name in the title or have the company name text on the page. This seems very unusual, but it is how Google is right now.

It may seem a bid odd, but many people still do searches for domain names in a search engine instead of typing the domain into the address bar in Internet Explorer. Someone might do a search for Amazon in Google instead of just putting in amazon.com in the Internet Explorer address bar. Because of this, it is important that you have your company name as text on each page.

Header Text

Text near top of your page is more significant to Google than text buried at bottom of page. Slightly larger text will most likely be more highly regarded by Google than smaller text. Using <h1> <h2> <h3> or larger text and putting your choice keywords near top of the page may help your ranking for these words.

Another thing worth mentioning is that Google may not use the Meta Tag description, so in your search result ranking, you will see a title and below it, you might just see random text pulled from text near the top of a page usually. As a result, you may want to put a readable line of text at the top of the page so that it will show up in the search ranking as something readable as opposed to random words.

See the example in Meta Tag section below for example of header text being indexed by Google.

Meta Tags

Although, most agree that Google isn't using Meta tags for rating purposes, they are using Meta tags now for description in search results for some sites. Make sure you put a meta tag for description on each webpage. Below is an example of a meta tag which is sometimes used by Google:

<meta name="description" content="Stock investment and news site">

It is important that your meta-tag description is something that is descriptive of your website and makes it look user friendly. As mentioned, this is not for rating purposes, but will show user what your site is about before they click on it. So, don't load it up with keywords or people may not click on it because it will look like spam to them.

Below is an example from wc3 website. When doing a search for wc3 in Google, it isn't pulling from the meta tag description. If it did use meta description, it would be right below the title in the search results. Below is the meta tag description and the Google results:

<meta name="description" content="W3C's nearly 400 member organizations lead the World Wide Web to its full potential. Founded by Tim Berners-Lee, the Web's inventor. The W3C Web site hosts specifications, guidelines, software and tools. Public participation is welcome. W3C supports universal access, the semantic Web, trust, interoperability, evolvability, decentralization, and cooler multimedia." >

Web | Images | Groups | News | Froogle | **more »**

`wc3` | Search

Web

Results **1** - **10** of

World Wide Web Consortium
Leading the Web to Its Full Potential... ...
www.w3.org/ - 26k - Jun 24, 2004 - Cached - Similar pages

Here is the top of W3C's website below. Notice the text *Leading the Web to Its Full Potential.* This is the text that Google is using in place of meta description tag. This is a perfect example of why first few lines of text are important near the top of the page. This becomes the description for your website to people who may have never been to your website before.

W3C WORLD WIDE WEB *c o n s o r t i u m*.

Leading the Web to Its Full Potential...
Activities | Technical Reports | Site Index | New Visitors | About W3C | Join W3C | Contact W3C

One thing worth mentioning is that Google is not always pulling one set of search results for particular sites. In the example above I have misspelled w3c to wc3 in Google. Wc3 shows search result as show above. Doing a search for the correctly spelled word w3c displays an indexed meta tag description result as opposed to the result above. They both have the same date next to them so they have been indexed on same day.

Google Hacks Exposed

As you can see in example directly above, the meta description tag in the source code matches what Google is showing in its search results. This is what you ideally want to have, but it will not always happen. So, it is good to be prepared for if it is indexed and if it is not indexed.

It is still unknown why some sites meta descriptions are not indexed. The W3C example is a great example. W3C is the standards board for some of the internet's leading technologies. They set guidelines for all sorts of things such as HTML, XML, etc. Its members include people from top tech companies to top university individuals. W3C has the highest PR available, 10.

If indexing meta tag descriptions is something that must be earned through good behavior, then W3C certainly deserves it. Yet, as I have shown, for one of the search terms used they have not been indexed.

Body Text

Text in your page is very important. In the past keyword density was listed as top priority for good ranking. Although this isn't the case as much anymore; it is still important to be clear with keywords near the top of the page and not have too many filler keywords such as and, the, it, was and other non-descriptive words.

In your body text, you can describe your products and services in a list with keywords as opposed to writing sentences describing everything. So for example you could do something like:

Specializing in:

- **Linux servers**
- **Computer workstations**
- **Consulting**

Then you could make these keywords links to your other pages and go on it detail below describing them.

It is still worth repeating keywords in your page. I've seen cases where someone that owns a domain to a keyword not even coming up first in the results because someone else has a webpage that lists the keyword more times.

Links

Links on your page are important for ranking. If your site is going to be considered a quality site, it will most likely be more than just one page and will have links to some outside links as well as having others link to it. Just having links isn't going to be as effective as having keyword targeted links.

Having a link that says "click here" isn't going to be as effective as "mp3 players" if mp3 is what you are selling for instance.

Some sites are breaking up large articles into many pages so that they can get more ads in for each page. Some have links such as Page1, Page2, and Page3 at bottom of the article with each of them being a separate link.

A more effective way of doing this would be to do: Page 1 – Review of X578 Player, Page 2 – MP3 Player Conclusion, etc. This example includes valuable keywords in the links which will make these pages look more important to Google.

Besides internal links to your pages, getting other sites to link to your site is very important.

Sites Linking to Your Site

Getting other sites to link to yours is really the next step that you need to take to improve your rank with Google. If your site is important, others will want to share it with people and will link to it. All important sites have outside links to them. And, the more important a site gets, the more links it has. Most of the PR10 sites have 10,000 or more links to them. A website cannot be an island without any links to it and expect to be ranked highly.

A good start to getting links to your site is to get listed in Yahoo directory, Dmoz.com, and business.com. These are all categorized directories. Once your site gets picked up by these directories it will get picked up by many other sites. This should help your ranking and also bring you a little traffic from these sources.

Big sites that have a high PR are good sites to have to link to your site. As mentioned above, directories are good, but news sites are also good. Putting out a press release and having a big news site link to you is a great and low cost way of getting others to link to you. Sites like http://www.prfree.com/ will send your press release out to many different news sources for free. Simply put a link to your website in the press release and you might get picked up by some big news sites as well as print news publishers.

When you get others to link to your site, make sure it isn't just an image link and that link covers some keywords if possible. Having a link that only highlights your company domain name doesn't do as much as if someone were to create a link on both company name and keyword. Investment World stock market news & advice isn't the same as: Investment World - stock market news & advice. The second example covers valuable keywords which should help. The first example only has a link with two words in it which may not be as effective as the second example.

Another way of getting someone to link to your site is to create a link to a script on your webpage with some text that reads something like, "please link to my site." Then simply post the html code they need to cut & paste. This is a simple and efficient way of getting people to link to your site.

In the past, people figured this out and would link trade with other sites. There are even software programs built around this. You put a link on your page and then email other sites and kindly ask them to put a link to your site from their site. Then, hopefully this will bring up your ranking up with Google.

Well, now it has changed a little. Links are still important, but every link isn't worth the same. Links to your site from link pages may hurt you and links for low PR sites may hurt you. A new trend now is getting someone with high a PR to link to your site. This will hopefully bring up your site's PageRank.

Also, having too many outgoing links to other sites starts to make your site look like a link site and may bring down your PR. Keeping outgoing links to minimum while keeping others linking to your site is what you optimally want.

Putting Google issue aside, having others link to your site is an important way of getting steady streams of traffic to your site. If you find a site out there that is useful and relevant to your site, it may be good to have them link to your site even if they have lower PR rating than your site. This might possibly lower your PR rank, but traffic from non search engine sources is important. Getting a good ranking with Google is important, but so is getting traffic to your site. Your Google ranking may go up and down over time, but links may stay forever. Getting people to link to your site will create steady traffic which is something that is not as easy to do with search engines.

A highlight on Anchor Text

This section is to stress the importance of the text that other sites use to link to your site. The link text that other sites use to link to your site (anchor text) is what search engines use to rank your site in many cases.

Take the Google bombing cases such as "miserable failure" hack and nowhere in the #1 site, George Bush homepage do you see the word "miserable failure". It is the anchor text that tells Google how to rate "miserable failure" in this case. With many other Google bombing cases, the anchor or link text is the sole determiner of how a site is ranked.

And, nowhere else on the George Bush page title, meta tags, domain name do you see anything close to the word "miserable failure."

It is simply the number of sites linking to the George Bush website and the link text that they all use that make George Bush the king of "miserable failure" in Google.

http://www.v7n.com/anchor_text_inbound_links.php

Linking to Other Sites

Since many people are concerned about Page Rank, you may not want to make your webpage look like a link site by having too may outside links. Too many outside links might lower your PR.

If you are an affiliate marketer and need to link to outside URL's, you may not want to link to the regular URL. You may want to use another method such as masking the link in a .php or .asp link.

PHP and ASP links are a great way of linking to a URL without making it look so obvious. So, instead of linking to http://outsidedomain.com you would link to http://yoursite.com/site1.php Then, you create a file called site1.php which does a redirect or meta refresh to http://outsidedomain.com .

The php code for site1.php looks like

```
<meta http-equiv="refresh"
content="0;URL=http://outsidedomain.com">
```

This is all that is in the file. When a user clicks on your site1.php link, they will be taken to the outsidedomain.com. However, to the search engine it probably isn't treated the same as a normal link to http://outsidedomain.com. Search engines often don't index php and asp as regularly or as well as simple html pages. This is fine because you would probably prefer that outside domains don't get indexed anyways.

You may get some sites that email you requesting that you link to their site and they will give you a link in return. You will want to make sure it is a fair link trade or you shouldn't do it. Some site owners will request that you link to their main website but are only willing to list your link in a separate link page which is on a totally separate domain with hundreds of other links. You probably don't want to link to sites like this. If someone wants a good link on your website, you should expect that they will do the same for you and not bury the link someplace where nobody will see it.

Images

In the future search engines will be able to read text on images. Most likely this will start out with the ability to pull keywords from an image on a simple solid background color.

In the future, image search may allow full page images to be indexed by search engines. When complex fonts and logos can be indexed by search engines, this will be a very big deal for search engine optimization.

In order to take advantage of image searches, it is important that you name your images with keywords such as nissian-altima.jpg instead of image1.jpg or image2.jpg.

While doing image searches in Google or Yahoo, you may notice that some very simple pictures come up that have text embedded into the picture. This does not mean that Yahoo or Google has ability to read text on images. If you look at most of these images, you will probably see that the text on the image does not match up with your search term. Rather, the image name and keywords on page match up with the keyword you searched for.

The reason that some spammers are creating image squares

with keywords embedded into the image most likely has to do with file size and to work with the doorway page scripts they have created.

If all images are the same exact size on a particular site, the uniqueness is low and that could be penalized by Google. When keywords are embedded into images, it changes the image file size for that particular image. Due to colors and changes in pixels or dots in an image, the size may be different for each image. By having keywords on an image it appears to be unique to search engines because of different image file names and file sizes.

On your webpage you will also want some text on your page that is similar to your image name. So, you may want to also have text on a site that says Nissan Altima if your image name is nisan-altima.jpg if you want to grab some searches for that particular keyword.

Page names may also go with this to be nissian-altima.html. If done properly, someone will do an image search on Yahoo Images or Google Images and see your picture come up. Google and Yahoo include a link to your website next to the image which will allow web surfers to go to your site.

This is just one more trick you can do to gain traffic.

Duplicate Pages

Duplicate websites on Google become un-indexable. If you copy someone else's website and leave most of the website the same and change just a few things, then when Google indexes it, it will most likely ignore your site.

If you do a search for your domain name in Google and you simply see the domain name for the search result with nothing besides it such as text describing the site, then you are a victim of Google's duplicate content filter.

It will stay this way until you change your website significantly from the site you copied it from.

Page Redirects

On Google webpage redirections are treated very much like duplicate webpages. When you do a search for a site that has been redirected, you may often just get the domain name with nothing else. This means that Google doesn't value it very much.

There are many different types of redirections that can be done. It can be done via server side or client side. Redirections can be done through web server software such as Apache or IIS on Windows platforms. On the server side, mod_rewrite may also be used to redirect pages.

On the client side, meta refresh can be done in html pages to redirect pages, and php or asp scripts can redirect pages also.

If you are trying to optimize your webpages you should not do redirects from your main domains because of these reasons.

Image alt tags

This is something that was abused in the past, but is still better than nothing. An image alt tag is a little box that pops up with text when you hold the mouse curser over an image. Image alt tags make browsing more user friendly for users and are something that is visible by end user. That is why it is important to try and add these to your images.

Below is example of an image alt tag. Notice the little box that says Yahoo next to curser. This is the alt tag.

Yahoo! Mail - New and improved. Get 100MB of storage and 10MB atl

Adding loads and loads of keywords probably isn't going to help, but a few words or descriptive sentence will make it better for the end user and may even bring up your search engine ranking.

Img alt tags are searchable by Google. If you type in the name of an alt tag, some sites will pop up that have that text in the image alt tag.

Checking out Your Competitors

Typing in some keywords into Google and learning about your competitors can be a very rewarding. There are some very aggressive marketers on the internet that use very interesting methods in order to get ranked highly.

What works on Yahoo's search engine may not work on Google. And what works on Microsoft Internet Explorer may not work with Mozilla web browser.

Because of this, it is important that you have some tools available when you are doing your research. The latest copies of Internet Explorer, and Mozilla Firefox (http://mozilla.org) are a must. If you want to add to the functionality of Internet Explorer you should try MyIE2 (http://myie2.com). MyIE2 is now called Maxthon. MyIE2 features tabbed browsing and a popup blocker. Mozilla Firefox also comes with a popup blocker and tabbed browsing. These things are important when you are researching aggressive marketers because there will be many popups.

Some of the webpages that spammers use are made specifically for Internet Explorer browsers. As a result of this, popups and redirects may only work if you are using Internet Explorer. MyIE2 runs using IE core, so the same issues you get with Internet Explorer you will most likely get with MyIE2.

This is where Mozilla Firefox comes in handy. When redirects are optimized for Internet Explorer, you may be able to browse a spammer's page with Mozilla Firefox and see the spammer's page that he/she is showing search engines. If you try the same page with Internet Explorer, you may see a brief glimpse of this page's background color before being redirected the page spammer wants you to see. With Mozilla you may see the entire page without getting redirected.

Sometimes, both browsers will be redirected to the spammer's page. In this case, you may want to use an offline web browser to retrieve pages. You can find offsite web browsers by doing search on download.com for offline browsers. You may also want to try a very old text based browser such as Lynx. Lynx only reads text and doesn't support redirects and many of the new things that most modern browsers· support. An online version of Lynx can be found at http://www.delorie.com/web/lynxview.html.

For offsite browsers you will simply right click on the spammer's page in Yahoo or Google search engine and put this URL into the offsite browser to retrieve the page. This should then download pages so you can see what spammer is showing search engines. You may need to go mimic the web browser by making sure that offsite browser is using a user agent that is similar to Internet Explorer.

Once these pages are downloaded, you can checkout their pages source code and see what they have done to get ranked so highly. Some of them don't want you to see these pages. If you put their URL into a web browser you may get an error message. Yet, the same URL may work when you click on it from the Google search results link.

What this means is that they are using web server software redirection such as mod_rewrite for Apache web server. They are putting in certain referral urls such as google.com, yahoo.com etc, and pointing all others to the error page.

Once you have their pages, you can investigate the number of links they have on pages, number of outside links that they link to etc.

If you find something that looks like a doorway page, you are probably seeing the page that is being shown to the search engine bots. However, if you don't see something like a doorway page, you may want to check the cache link next to the search results link. The spammer might be cloaking so that only if you

Google bot IP or user agent can see their page. However, if page has been cached, you will see exactly what search engine bot saw when it indexed the site.

You will also probably want to have a program that will trace IP addresses of websites. VisualRoute (http://visualware.com) integrates into the web browser and is great for this task. Simply put in the website URL into the program and it will trace it back to server giving you name of ISP (internet service provider) IP address of the server the website is hosted on and whois or name info of the person that owns the domain.

This information will be valuable to you in figuring out what other websites spammer is using and provide technical details such as IP's spammer is using. These things will also be valuable if you decide to report these people to Google. If you can find some of spammers' other domains, it may make investigation by Google a little easier.

You will most likely not get the correct name, company or phone number of the spammer because many people don't list the correct info on their domains because it makes them too available to mail, telephone and email solicitors. The email address will most likely be working, however.

This info is not needed anyways in order to report to Google. Simply the URL of the search result and a little bit of other information is all that is needed.

Differences between Yahoo and Google Cache

It appears that Yahoo is keeping a cache of about twelve indexes. Basically what it looks like Yahoo is doing is indexing a site and shortly after doing around twelve more indexes.

I am guessing that this is the case because one of the dynamic pages I checked in Yahoo had about 12 screenshots listed in its cache link.

If you look at cache of certain domains on Yahoo, you may see cache of around twelve pages. You will only see this on dynamic doorway pages. These pages upon refresh display new keywords on the page and background color. Regular sites will most likely show just one cached page on Yahoo. On Google only one cached page is shown for all sites.

What this means is that it looks like Yahoo is going to start penalizing dynamic doorway pages as Google has done. Any page that shows more than one page in cache will most likely start being penalized or dropped by Yahoo.

As mentioned, dynamic doorway pages used to be monopolizing many search terms in Google, but they put a stop to that. Now dynamic doorway pages don't show up very much on Google.

Most of these dynamic pages can only be found now in Google by doing a search for their domain names. Typing in the domain in Google for one of these dynamic websites will usually show only the domain name without any description text in the search results. Even doing a search for their page titles they can usually not be found. This means that they are most likely penalized or are blacklisted by Google.

Another thing worth mentioning is that when you do a search for a domain name in Google; try it with and without the www in front of it. You may notice different results.

Protecting your site: Hurting your competition

In competitive industries business can be ruthless. Companies are fighting for same customers everyday. There are ways that you can damage your competitors discretely without them knowing and gain from their loss.

If one of your competitors sites go down or they have dead links on site, you may submit their dead pages or website URL to the search engine. Then, search engine may index their website a little faster and catch the problems and bring their ranking down lower.

Or, if your competitors are advertising on Google Adwords or Overture, feel free to click on their ads for their high priced ad words. Those ads clicks might be costing them $5 per click!

If it ends up costing them too much to advertise, they may stop using that keyword which will give you room to take over and start advertising for that keyword at a lower rate, possibly.

If your competitor is cheating Google or hurting your company by misusing your trademarks or URL, you can report them to Google.

http://www.google.com/contact/spamreport.html

Here is some list of problems that Google has listed on its abuse page:

Hidden text or links
Misleading or repeated words
Page does not match Google's description
Cloaked page
Deceptive redirects
Doorway pages
Duplicate site or pages
Other (specify)

Google states following:

"Google will investigate each report and will take action if abuse is uncovered."

Some more ruthless things you could do to damage your competitors are as follows:

1. Submit them to link farms
2. Create link to them with keyword and "worst" or "spam" at a link site
3. Create link or Page Title with competitor name or URL in it to another site

Of course, you don't want to do any of these things from your main site or affiliated sites or you can expect that they may start doing the same things to your site.

1. When you are submitting them to link farm, you are not helping their link popularity. You are probably hurting it. And, this page might get pulled up in search rank for someone who is searching for something on your competitor. Then, some non relevant link page might get listed higher than their company site.

2. Creating links with words like worst, rip-off or spam will make your competitors look bad. Especially if a user does a search on competitor or puts in the website name in Google, then people may see a page with the title "Worst Company Ever" for title and then the horror story in description. This certainly will not make your competitor look very good.

A good example of this is Paypal. Do a search for "paypal" in Google. At the top of the ranking is PayPal's site, and a few below that is PayPal Sucks.com and then a PayPalWarning.com. For someone looking at Paypal for the first time as a payment provider, this does not look good to them. Or, if a customer is thinking of switching, something like this might be enough for them to drop Paypal upon seeing it.

Some other things that spammers may do that is very annoying is having a software popup box that comes up when you go to a website. These boxes popup and ask you to install some software. When you go to cancel it, it keeps popping up.

Another thing that some sites do that is very bad is to eliminate back button function on browser. After going to the site, when you click on back button it goes to their site and keeps you from escaping. Then you have to go to back history dropdown in order to escape or close browser.

These are some additional things that you may want to report to Google's abuse site.

Google paypal Search Adv. Pref

Web

PayPal
Service allows visitors to send money and bills to anyone with e-mail, auctions, classified
ites,...
www.**paypal**.com/ - Similar pages

www.paypal.com/cgi-bin/webscr?cmd=p/gen/about-outside
Similar pages
[More results from www.paypal.com]

ttps://www.paypal.com/
Similar pages

www.x.com/
Similar pages

www.paypal.co.uk/
Similar pages

PayPalSucks.com is where you will learn the abuse, fraud, & evil ...
PayPal used to be the best thing on the web. ... Wednesday, 21-Apr-2004 21:55:14 MST.
Welcome to NoPayPal! So, what's wrong with **PayPal** and why is this site here? ...
www.**paypal**sucks.com/ - 21k - Apr 21, 2004 - Cached - Similar pages

PaypalWarning.com - **Paypal** Warning to Investors, Merchants, ...
PaypalWarning.com is in no way affiliated with **Paypal**, Inc. **PayPal**, Inc. 1840
Embarcadero Rd Palo Alto CA 94303. **PayPal**, Inc. ...
www.**paypal**warning.com/ - 15k - Cached - Similar pages

Tongkat Ali, unrestricted sex – **PayPal**, restricted account

For those of you concerned about your company name and
reputation, buying up these domains such as
"yourcompanynamesucks.com" may keep this from happening.
Did you know that George Bush bought bushsucks.com and
about 200 others? Or did you know that NAACP purchased the

Google Hacks Exposed

"n" word domain? They did it to protect their reputation and to prevent someone from abusing their website. These websites will most likely never be used by them, but they purchased them so that nobody else can use them.

http://www.wired.com/news/politics/0,1283,19703,00.html
http://www.wired.com/news/culture/0,1284,21873,00.html

Unicode

The use of Unicode in your page title is another hack that may make your site stand out. What is Unicode you may be asking? Unicode is the code for special characters such as arrows, copyright symbols and other things.

Unicode will usually not show up correctly in most internet browsers. It will most likely display a question mark instead of symbol in your browser title bar. However, in some search engines the symbols are readable. When properly setup users will see arrows or stars next to your page title in the search results. Here is example of right arrow in action from Yahoo search engine.

16. ▶▶ CANEage.com :: Games, Betas, Modding, Hardware, Tweakin▪ & CANEing 📑
... Write a review for ►► CANEage.com. Please enter information according to the specifications ... 2) 1 **Star** (1) 1/2 **Star**. This product's score ... www.caneage.com/modules.php? op=modload&name=Reviews&file=index&req=write_review&POSTNUKESID=2d4e 0 - 26k - Cached

Here is what it looks like on the website: Notice that it only shows two squares instead of the right arrows. This is because Unicode is not readable in browsers but only by certain search engines.

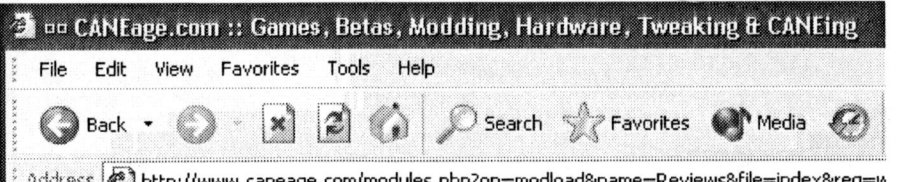

This makes your site stand out from others in the search rankings. And, if you are at the bottom of the list that star next to your page name may be what it takes to get people to click on it.

As these symbols became popular, Google stopped showing some of them in search results. Many still work, though, and some that don't show up in the search engine rankings may show up properly in Google directory.

A common and attractive looking one is #9658; this code when put in the page title displays a right arrow. This one doesn't work anymore in Google. However, star works in Yahoo search. The code for star is &#9733. Simply put this in the page title area so that it looks like this:

<title>&#9733 Your title</title>

This will display a star in front of the title Yahoo in the Yahoo search engine. Here is what it looks like when it is working:

YAHOO! search | star in title google | | Yahoo

| **Web** | **Images** | **Directory** | **Yellow Pages** | **News** | **Products** |

TOP 20 WEB RESULTS   out of about 575,000. Search took 0.09 seconds. (What's this?)

1. dark-**star**.joeuser.com - Article Referrals 🗐
   ... Dark-**Star's** Place. My Favorites ... 41575 Referral(s) from the 1170 link(s) below: **Title**: Go
   Search: what goes around comes around ...
   dark-star.joeuser.com/referrals.asp?cmd=showSiteReferralDetails&dname=google.com - 526k
   Cached - More pages from this site

2. ★ Using a **star in** your **title** 🗐
   ... 9733; Using a **star in** your **title**. Saw a site do it and am in two minds of ... meant to decyp
   HTML codes but obviously **Google** picks up on it ...
   www.webmasterworld.com/forum3/16326.htm - More pages from this site

One thing that is quite interesting is that you can do a search in Yahoo for "star in title Google" or for "9733 in title Google". They both point to same page, but one shows a star and the other one shows 9733 instead of a star.

You can also put Unicode in the body of your webpage or in your meta description tag. It appears as black star in search results when you do this.

The thing is it only appears that star appears now in yahoo when specifically searching for star. If you don't search for a star, it specifies Unicode.

Here is another one that works in Yahoo:

Notice the sunshine image next to the text Google Indicateur? A closer look at the title tag shows how this is done: <title>☼ Google Indicateur   </title>

You may still be able to find some Unicode that will work with Google. It is really a cat & mouse strategy to drawing attention to your site. Unicode that becomes too popular will be removed by Google. Just be aware that this strategy changes all the time.

Some of you that have used the World Wide Web for a while may remember blinking text on websites. This was done by simply using putting <blink> your text </blink> into the html on your webpage. After so many people started using this it became annoying to many. So, it was removed from newer versions of Internet Explorer. Now it only works on Netscape or Mozilla based browsers. This is sort of the same thing with Unicode. If it becomes too annoying, Google will most likely stop it.

Here is a link displaying all of the Unicode icons.

http://www.unicode.org/charts/PDF/U2600.pdf

Page Updates

Keep your pages updated. Make sure every so often you update your site. Even if your site is #1 on Google for a search word, if you don't update it for 6 months, you will probably drop off the list. The Google algorithm most likely checks the file size of your pages for changes. If the file size stays the same all the time then it is stale and will lower your ranking.

Some spammers took advantage of this in the past and created dynamic doorway pages that upon refreshing would load entirely new doorway pages with different background colors and new keywords. To the search engines it must have appeared that they really had some fresh content because it was always new whenever the spider re-indexed the site. And, every second the site could be considered new. Simply refreshing the page loaded a new page.

Most legitimate dynamic pages do not even update this often, so now or in the future one might expect that the Google spider may spider sites and then shortly after do a quick spider right after this to see if things change. If a site is different, after doing this a handful of times, then the site might be removed from the index.

Google has basically removed these spammers but many of them still exist on the Yahoo search engine.

Robots.txt

If you monitor your log files you may notice a lot of links to robots.txt. Robots.txt is a file that you can use to tell search engines what you want to exclude from being indexed.

Some search engines may obey this while others may disobey it. For instance, if you want to keep search engine bots out from folders /images and /cgi-bin you could put the following in the robots.txt file:

```
User-agent: *
Disallow: /cgi-bin/
Disallow: /images/
```

Simply put this file in your root web directory for your domain and that is it.

You shouldn't think of robots.txt as a security measure because it is not. If you have info that you do not want the public to see, you will have to password protect it. Here is an example, do a search for robots.txt in Google and whitehouse.gov is listed near the top. Below is example of this robots.txt. This might be embarrassing to have something like this for your site as the

Whitehouse has. It appears as though you are trying to cover things up and makes the website look suspicious. This is especially the case with the whitehouse.gov one.

robots.txt for http://www.whitehouse.gov/

```
User-agent:                            *
Disallow:                         /cgi-bin
Disallow:                         /search
Disallow:                      /query.html
Disallow:                          /help
Disallow:                    /360pics/iraq
Disallow:                    /360pics/text
Disallow:                /911/911day/iraq
Disallow:                /911/911day/text
Disallow:                /911/heroes/iraq
Disallow:                /911/heroes/text
Disallow:                      /911/iraq
Disallow:              /911/patriotism/iraq
Disallow:              /911/patriotism/text
Disallow:             /911/patriotism2/iraq
Disallow:             /911/patriotism2/text
Disallow:                /911/progress/iraq
Disallow: /911/progress/text
```

There is also a meta-tag code for robots also. If you don't want search engines to show the cache of the site to the public, put this into the meta-tag.

```
<META NAME="ROBOTS" CONTENT="NOARCHIVE">
```

You can find out more below or by doing search for robots.txt

http://www.searchengineworld.com/robots/robots_tutorial.htm

Password Protected Pages

Password protected pages cannot be indexed by search engines. So, if you have a password protected page where username/password box pops up when you try to access the site, then it cannot be accessed by search engines.

PDF Files

Adobe Acrobat PDF files are not generally indexed well if at all by search engines. Avoid using PDF files on your website for most things. Not only is it bad for search engines, but the files take a long time to load and can cause other applications to lock up.

Google claims it can index PDF files but other search engines may not be able to index them as well. So try avoiding PDF files.

http://www.searchenginestrategies.biz/websiteoptimizationpdffiles.htm

http://www.google.com/webmasters/facts.html

Flash Files

Flash and Shockwave files are also not indexable by search engines. Some of the links may be indexed within flash, but search engines cannot read the images and media content within flash files.

As a result of this, don't expect to make an entire website based on Flash and have search engines pick it up. You will need to have alternative text based pages so that they can be indexed properly.

The same is so for video files. The only thing in a video that is going to be indexed is the filename of the video. Search engines cannot index anything inside of the video.

Framed Pages

Framed pages have historically had problems with search engines. Most sources will tell you to avoid frames if possible. If you have to use frames, create a no frames reference and/ or links to pages in the frames.

http://www.searchenginestrategies.biz/websiteoptimizationframe s.htm

Top PR Sites

Google PageRank plays an important role in determining how important a site is. PR is measured on a scale of 0-10 with 0 being worst and 10 best. Here are some top PR sites which were compiled on April 24, 2004

10: Google, Real, Apple, MIT, Macromedia, NASA
9: Yahoo, Microsoft, USAToday, MP3.com, Standford.edu
8: Dell, Wired, GM,

You can find Pagerank by downloading Google toolbar and going to the site you want to look at. When you move the cursor over the Page Rank bar it will show the PR number. In the example below, yahoo.com has a rating of 10 which is the best.

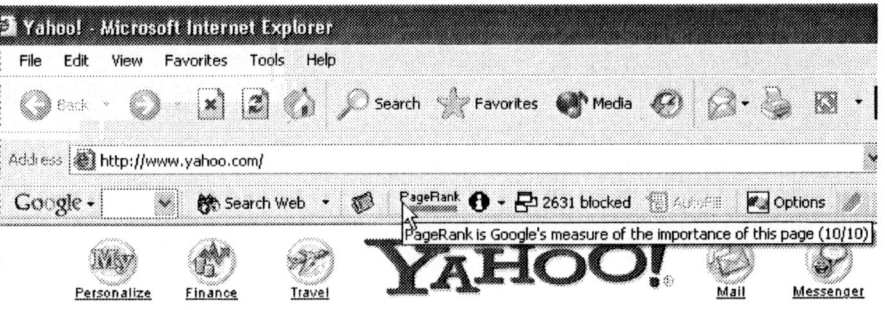

The PR changes in the toolbar window as you go from site to site. Front pages usually always have a PR. However secondary pages or websites with very little traffic may not have a PR yet.

 Be aware that most of the high ranking sites don't have popup windows or redirects. And, all of the PR 10 sites listed have zero popups.

Most of the PR 10 sites have lots of sites linking to them with usually around 30,000 or more sites linking to them. An exception is keio.ac.jp which only has approx 2,300 sites linking to it.

Some other interesting things to note are that not all pages rank very well. Usually only top level pages get PR. Also, some sites don't do well with PR. Database backend sites like shopping sites usually don't have a PR for lots of pages and if they do, it is much lower than other type of non-database sites. Take Bestbuy.com for example. They have PR of 9 on main site, but all other pages have PR 0 or aren't ranked.

http://www.acroterion.ca/Knowledge-Base-Top-Sites-With-PageRank-10.html

How is Page Rank Calculated?

$$PR(A) = (1-d) + d(PR(t1)/C(t1) + ... + PR(tn)/C(tn))$$

This was the original formula for Page Rank developed by Google's founders while in Stanford. It has most likely changed since then, but this is the only published formula that is known.

What does this mean?

In the equation 't1 - tn' are pages linking to page A, 'C' is the number of outbound links that a page has and 'd' is a damping factor, usually set to 0.85. A page's Page Rank = 0.15 + 0.85 * (a "share" of the Page Rank of every page that links to it)

Basically the formula is a combination of number of outbound links, PR of sites linking to yours and the number of sites linking to yours determines your PR. More info can be found at the link below.

http://www.webworkshop.net/pagerank.html

Search Engine Submission Process

When submitting your site to Google, it is important to make sure it is done the right way or it may cost you a good rank.

With just a single domain, the submission process is pretty straightforward. Simply go to Google's webpage and submit the domain name to Google. There is no need to try and submit independent pages because submitting the main domain will index all of your pages that are linked to it.

However, with multiple domains, you may want to be more careful. If your sites are all independent from one another and don't have links to one another, you can just submit them the normal way.

If you are submitting other domains to try to improve the rank of one of your sites and are linking pages to one another, it is important that you don't just go and submit them all together at the same time from the same place. The reason for this is that you are trying to make your sites appear as independent sites that just happen to link to one another. If you submit them all at once, it will appear to Google that they are all part of the same group and are connected to one another or to the same owner. This is not what you want.

As mentioned, you need links from outside sources. Some of the domains that you are submitting are supposed to be outside sources. You need to make them appear as if they are even though they are not. Instead of submitting all sites at the same time, submit the main site, and then indirectly submit other sites through the grapevine.

You might be saying, well, my domains are all on separate IP addresses and if I use different internet connections and submit them the same day they will appear as if they are separate.

This is wrong. When you think about how natural websites grow up, all of the sites don't just popup right away. A site is submitted, it takes some time, people find out about it. People start linking to sites only after they have been around for a while. So, wait some time to submit your other sites or submit it to an outside domain which will then be re-indexed by Google which will notice your pages and index them.

Another option is just to have links to some of your other domains from one of your sites. Then, Google should find it and index it.

New Domains vs. Existing Domains

As mentioned above, when submitting domains to search engines, you do not want to have all of your sites that link to one another to be submitted all at the same time. If you are trying to make your domains appear to be independent from one another, it is important that you make the process seem as natural as process to the search engine. What you don't want is all your sites to immediately light up for the first time on Google as though an entire neighborhood of Christmas lights goes up for the first time all together.

The evolution of websites is most likely not one that is instantaneous. Websites are created and submitted at all different times. Microsoft.com, Dell.com and others didn't all get on to the web at exactly the same time.

For this reason what some people are doing is buying other's existing domains that have already been indexed by Google and changing the site to a doorway page site

Since the domain has already been indexed by Google, it already appears to be independent from your sites and can be changed to meet your needs.

And, a plus is that some of these expiring domains also may still have some traffic going to them.

The alternative to buying used domains is to buy new, un-used domains. These domains haven't been indexed by search engines and will take longer to get linked up with your other sites on Google.

For this reason, existing domains will be much quicker getting up for the "Army of Sites" concept. Refer to "Army of Sites" section of this book for more info on this.

Google is not perfect for all sites

Another problem is that the Google algorithm isn't perfect. It currently doesn't work well with all types of sites. News type and high content type sites do much better with Google than outside link pages or sites with little internal content. Although for most sites, this is probably good thing, there are some sites out there that are incredibly useful to people and have little internal content. Because of this, they show poor PR rankings with Google.

A great example of this is adult sites and TGP sites to be more specific. TGP stands for thumbnail gallery post. Webmasters typically make galleries with pictures and videos on them and submit them to TGP sites. Then, the end user browses the TGP site which has links or picture links to all of the free galleries.

Lots of these TGP sites will require that people link to their site in their pages in order to get listed on their TGP. One of the largest TGP sites is thehun.net. It is ranked as 1015st most popular site on web by Alexa. Thehun.net gets over 1 million unique people to visit its TGP site everyday. Thehun.net has approx 7500 sites that link to it.

The site is free of popups, has plenty of links to it, is very popular, and yet has a Google PR of only 5. The reason for this is that the site has mostly links to other sites and very little of its own content. And, many of the links to it are picture links which don't help too much. These sites linking too it also are low content, low PR pages as well.

A similar traffic site, fool.com features financial information for people. The site has an Alexa ranking of 1200, which means it gets a little less traffic than thehun.net. The site has approx 12000 sites that link to it. These links are more likely text links which help. Also the site features pages and pages of internal content. Fool.com has PR of 8.

In conclusion, high Google PR ranks will not always be possible for every type of site as Google currently is today.

Google Dance

Google dance is a term used to describe the index update of the Google search engine. Google is made up of thousands of computers which communicate with one another and spider websites. Google has many different data centers which handle search queries that people type in. Some of them are:

www.google.com
www2.google.com
www3.google.com
www-sj.google.com

Most of the time if you do a search for the same keyword, these data centers will display the same results. However, occasionally these results will be different. So, your website may appear #1 on one data center and may be in a different place in another data center page.

Even though your website may be spidered every few days by Google, your position on Google may not change for several days after this. Then, one of the Google data centers may update your position while some of the others may stay the same.

When this happens on the main Google website you may notice that if you do a refresh your search, you may see your placement in the search engine go up and down. This is called the Google Dance because the search result index is alternating between old and new results. Within a short period of time, the new index will go to all of Google data centers and the results will be consistent again.

Google Dance occurs because Google has tens of thousands of PC's that it uses. They are not all updated at the same time and they are not all working on the same tasks at the same time. When you notice a change between search results, you are witnessing Google's load balancing which alternates between datacenters or computer systems.

If one system gets too much traffic, you will be redirected to another system that does not have as much of a load on it. This all happens within seconds and you will hardly notice the difference most of the time when you are doing searches.

Some websites are available that will show you whether or not Google is in a dance period. Basically what the tool does is searches the same keyword within three different Google datacenters. If you see a difference between them, your website is in process of being re-ranked.

http://www.google-dance-tool.com/what_is_google_dance.html
http://www.google-dance-tool.com/#google_dance_tool

PHP/ASP Scripts and Google

Content Management Systems such as PHPNuke, Mambo, Postnuke and others are scripts that allow content rich websites to be quickly and easily updated. These scripts are typically based on php or asp. Php and asp are scripting languages that are typically used with database integrated sites.

PHP is typically used for UNIX/Linux servers and is open source or freely available. ASP is used typically with Windows based servers and is not open source. PHP usually integrates with MySQL databases and ASP typically integrates with Microsoft SQL Server databases.

Content management systems such as Mambo and PHP Nuke typically use strings for links so that a link on the site might look something like http://yourdomain.com/index.php?option=links These strings or question marks in the URL make it difficult for search engines to index these URLs.

As a result of this, some CMS (Content Management Systems) such as Mambo and others have search engine friendly URL options which allow the links to be re-done to something without the strings in the URL's.

Besides CMS systems you may have some other scripts which leave strings in the URL. These scripts may also have mods available to make the URL's friendlier to search engines.

This typically involves using a mod called mod_rewrite for Apache web server which rewrites the URL to something friendlier.

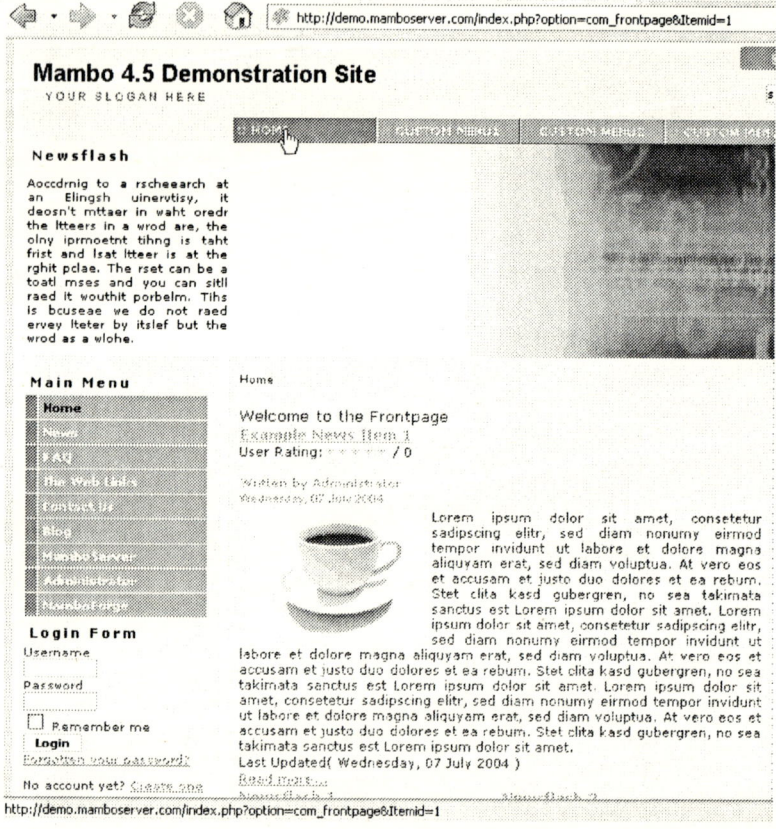

As you can see above, in the URL this particular site is not using search friendly URL's. To change to a search engine friendly URL, many CMS's such as Mambo have option to change URLs to search engine friendly URLs. See Mambo Admin picture below for example:

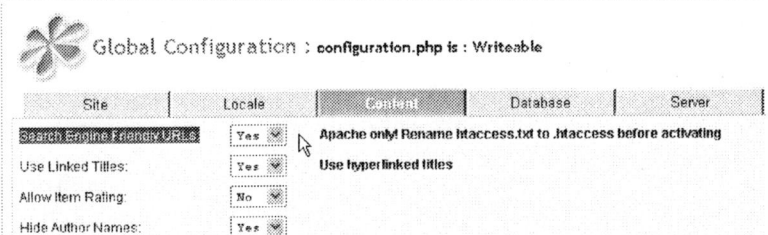

For more info on creating search engine friendly URL's checkout http://www.sitepoint.com/article/search-engine-friendly-urls/

Google Toolbar

When you download the Google toolbar and install it, you have the option to setup PageRank display. When you do so, a privacy warning pops up stating that the URL of sites you visit will be automatically forwarded to Google.

Alexa.com, a site that ranks website traffic uses similar method for calculating website traffic. Millions of people download the Alexa toolbar. When those people go to a website, it counts one hit or vote per website per day. Then, votes are sent back to Alexa which compiles the data for website traffic rankings.

Google Pagerank may be similar to this. Although most people are saying, that Google Pagerank is determined by relationships between sites and links to sites, this data sent from the Google toolbar users to Google may also play a role in determining how sites are ranked and/or Page Rank.

What are some of the things that the toolbar could possibly do? Well, first it tracks the sites you go to. If someone goes to your site and then to USA Today.com right after it, that might help your site if your site is similar to that. If people that visit USAToday visit your site within a close period of time, that might make your site more relevant for that topic. And, your site might show up under the similar pages link in search results for USAToday.

Also, if someone keeps going back to your website everyday or spends a long time there, that might help. And, if someone spends a short period of time on your site, that might hurt your ranking. If the Google toolbar is measuring the time spent on site that could make it very difficult for people to cheat.

In such a case, to cheat this type of system would take considerable resources. Software would have to be designed to act like an individual user and go to certain web pages and click on links on your pages. Besides that, most Google toolbar users are on different IP addresses. Cookies are also something that each user has installed. The system would have to have multiple IP addresses and manage cookies for each particular user. Of course there would just be one user, you but you would want to trick them to think that you are thousands or millions of people.

Or, instead of doing all of this, you could just spend the time to create a nice website and hope that you get ranked well.

Maximizing your traffic

Putting search engine and Google stuff aside, you have traffic and visitors going to your site that needs to be managed effectively. Below are some of the things for maximizing traffic:

Error Pages

Some people may try accessing areas of your site and may not be able to access anything. They may have mistakenly typed in the wrong page name, directory name or something similar.

If you don't have error pages setup, they will just get an ugly error page or nothing at all. You can stop this by setting up error pages for your web server. In Apache web server in your Virtual host area, you may add the following:

ErrorDocument 404 http://yourdomain.com/404.html
ErrorDocument 403 http:// yourdomain.com /403.html
ErrorDocument 500 http:// yourdomain.com/500.html

So, your virtual host directive for your website will look something like:

```
<VirtualHost *:80>
DocumentRoot "/var/www/html/ yourdomain.com "
ServerName yourdomain.com
ServerAlias *.yourdomain.com
CustomLog logs/yourdomain.com-access_log
ErrorDocument 404 http://yourdomain.com/404.html
ErrorDocument 403 http:// yourdomain.com /403.html
ErrorDocument 500 http:// yourdomain.com/500.html
</VirtualHost>
```

In the example above, whenever someone gets one of the following errors, they will go to the page you have specified above.

You could alternatively put something like this in your .htaccess file in the directory you want it to be active in.

These pages can go to a separate page, or you can put in your index.html page and have those all go to your main webpage.

You may also trade traffic with someone else and send them traffic from your error pages. Then, your traffic partner will send you traffic in return. By trading traffic you may increase your traffic or hopefully exchange your bad traffic for good traffic.

Directory Trick

If you are offering free pictures or videos to people, you may want to try this trick. Instead of putting an index.htm file in a directory, put your images on something like gallery.html. If you are offering free images from http://yourdomain.com/galleries/gallery.html you may get some sneaky people that will delete the gallery.html in their browser to point back to http://yourdomain.com/galleries/ They will do this with the hope that you will have more free pictures there.

If you have directory browsing turned off in Apache, when the user puts this in the URL, it will give them an error message which will pull up your error page document. This page you can have go to any URL. You can even have it load your sponsor's webpage or traffic trade partner.

So, you might even want to trade this traffic with a traffic trade partner. Since they are trying to take backdoor entrances, you may want to trade them with traffic from another source that is more valuable.

Leechers

If you are offering videos or pictures, you probably have some of these leechers. Other websites may be linking directly to your images or videos without going through your html pages first. The problem with this is that these people are less likely to convert to sales if they aren't seeing ads or seeing it the way you designed it to be.

So, you may have lots of people using up your bandwidth loading your videos and you getting nothing from it. You can put a stop to this with some simple code using an Apache module, mod_rewrite. Simply create an .htaccess file in a directory near where you have your content stored.

```
RewriteEngine on
RewriteCond %{HTTP_REFERER} !^$
RewriteCond                            %{HTTP_REFERER}
!^http://(www\.)?yourdomain.com(/)?.*$    [NC]
RewriteRule         .*\.(gif|jpg|jpeg|bmp|mpg|mpeg|avi|wmv)$
http://yourdomain.com/rightpage.html [R,NC]
```

Simply add this to an .htaccess file. In this example, if someone were to link directly to an image outside of yourdomain.com, they will get redirected to rightpage.html. Only yourdomain.com can link directly to images/videos and get away with it without seeing this error page or exit page come up.

This trick will hopefully convert some traffic into sales and/or save you on your bandwidth expenses.

Bookmark

Getting people to bookmark your website is a very important thing for many websites. The people that bookmark your site may keep coming back to your site and may refer others to your site.

So, once someone comes to your site, you may want to encourage them to bookmark your site by placing some text on your page telling them to bookmark the page. You can even create a script for this and create a link to it. Have them click a "bookmark this site" link and it will automatically load the bookmark menu in their browser.

Here is a script that when clicked will prompt the user to bookmark the site.

```
<a
href="javascript:window.external.AddFavorite('http://yoursite.com
', 'Your Site Name')">
    <img src=images/addfavorites.gif border="0" align="middle"
alt="Bookmark Yoursite.com"></a>
```

It is advised that you don't create an auto popup bookmark script. These are annoying and may possibly be considered spam. Also, don't do an auto-popup "make homepage" script. Most people are happy with their homepage link and would not want to switch their homepage from msn, yahoo, or Google to your site. Encouraging the bookmark is fine, however.

Some of the most valuable sites on the internet were built from bookmarking traffic. Sites like Yahoo and Google didn't have to advertise in order to get people going to their sites. Word of mouth and bookmarking is how people discovered these sites.

Bookmarking traffic is probably the most valuable traffic you can get. People will remember the name of your site once they bookmark it and come back and back again.

Tell a Friend Script

Besides having a bookmark script, you may also want to have a script that allows people to tell their friends & family about your site. Below is an example of this type of script.

Tell A Friend About This Web Site:

Your Name	
Your Email	
Friend's Name	
Friend's Email	
A Quick Note	
Tell Your Friend About This Site	

Privacy Info: Your information is private and NOT STORED. It is ONLY used to generate an email message.

This script above is a very simple one. There are many others available. Simply go to a script site such as http://hotscripts.com for other "tell a friend" scripts.

Favicon.ico

What is favicon.ico?

Favicon.ico is something you may see listed in your log files for your website. It is a name given to an icon that you may see when you bookmark or go to a website.

Essentially favicon.ico is a tiny image that is renamed with the .ico extension.

When someone bookmarks your site, if you have favicon.ico in your main webpage directory, an icon will show up in your browser in the address bar and in your bookmarks.

A good example of this is Yahoo or Google. Load their site into your browser and you will see a little picture in the address or

URL bar next to the URL. This helps users to identify and remember your site.

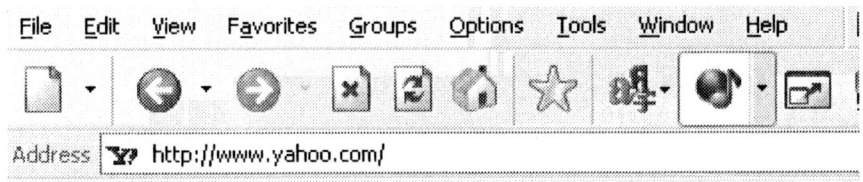

Notice the red Y icon next to the URL. That Y will also appear in the bookmarks folder.

Also, in the bookmarks file, it will help your site stand out from others which will increase your chances of someone clicking on your bookmark and going to the site. Many of your users may have fifty or more bookmarks in their bookmarks folder. Having a pretty icon next to your site will make your site easy to find for your viewers.

Favicon.ico files can be made by downloading a program that is designed for favicon.ico. A quick search for favicon will list some of the software programs.

DNS

Many sites don't seem to have DNS (Domain Name System) setup properly for websites which will annoy some users. The most basic setup should allow a user to type in domain.com or www.domain.com and reach your site. Some sites only have www.domain.com setup.

Having only www.domain.com setup may have made sense ten years ago when there were other popular protocols such gopher and things like that. Now, World Wide Web, www and the internet are pretty much thought of as the same thing. Allowing a user to access your site through either entry will make it easier for people to find your site.

And, don't forget, some sites may be trying to link to your site. If they accidentally leave off the www from your domain in your link, people won't be able access your site from that link if you don't have the DNS setup for yourdomain.com.

Your web host or webmaster should be able to make sure that you have both DNS entries put in properly.

Blogs

Blogs are a relatively new thing. Blogs are essentially online diaries or communities where people post articles and topics. They are usually cluttered and often cover a variety of issues.

Below is a blog called Poor Man. http://www.thepoorman.net/ Like most blogs it has many links to other blogs and sites.

Blogs have been used for Google bombing. The "weapons of mass destruction" hack was as a result of large numbers of blog sites linking to a specific site.

One of the largest blogs is called Blogger.com. It was recently purchased by Google for a large sum of money. This site allows people to create their own blogs free of charge.

Something that some people are now doing is creating lots of blogs and then pointing their blogs to one another. In each of these blogs is usually adult site links which they are affiliates of.

By doing these things, the PR of these sites will go up and may help them get ranked better on Google.

Google's blogger service Blogger.com does not allow the posting of obscene links or text, so many of these blogs are deleted by Google because nudity or adult material is considered to be obscene.

As a result of this, the use of Blogger.com is only a short term way of increasing PR if you are marketing adult websites.

http://www.wired.com/news/business/0,1367,64468,00.html
http://www.wired.com/news/business/0,1367,64422,00.html

Stealing Searches

There are some websites out there that are stealing search engine ratings from other sites. What some sites are doing is loading up pages with the domain names of sites such as competitorsite.com throughout the page. This is simply accomplished by placing text throughout a page that shows competitors site name and hyperlinks that have a competitor's site name in the link text.

After doing this, when someone searches for your competitor's site, your site may come up above their site in the search or may appear in the ranking near them.

This is a dirty trick but can be easily accomplished. Many people are competing over common keywords, but website names don't have as much competition. Most websites may only mention the name of their site a couple of times on each page or even less than that. This text is typically only found on owner's site, so there isn't a lot of competition for these keywords.

However, many people may be searching using the website name. Simply putting the site name throughout some of your pages will help get some additional traffic.

You must understand that by doing this, you could anger the person you are taking the website name from. This may be a trademarked or copyrighted name. It is possible that they could report you to Google and get you banned for this.

Report Cheaters

When you do a search for keywords for your website and you notice someone listed above you that is cheating, feel free to report those sites to Google. They can be reported here: http://www.google.com/contact/spamreport.html

After all, they are hurting the traffic to your site. Once they get removed, your site may move further up in rank. This is an easy & ethical way of boosting traffic to your site.

You are helping yourself, helping web surfers and improving Google's quality when you report cheaters.

Monitoring Your Progress

After your sites have been submitted to search engines such as Google, you will want to start monitoring your progress and see what is being indexed and how your ratings are for certain keywords.

In Google, you can do a search for allinurl: www.yourdomain.com site:www.yourdomain.com. Simply replace the yourdomain.com with whatever your domain name is. This particular search will see what Google has indexed from your site. The following is an example with cisco.com:

Web   Results **1 - 100** of about **227,0(**

Cisco Systems, Inc
Skip Navigation Skip to Content Skip to Search Skip to Footer. Cisco Systems, Inc.(R), Log
In | Register | Contacts & Feedback | Help ...
www.cisco.com/ - 55k - Aug 7, 2004 - Cached - Similar pages - Stock quotes: CSCO

Cisco Connection Documentation
Product Documentation. Routers ...
www.cisco.com/univercd/home/home.htm · 30k · Cached - Similar pages

New Page Location-Education in the Internet Economy - Cisco ...
... Please update your bookmarks. This page has a new page location:
http://**www.cisco.com**/en/US/learning/le42/le12/learning_networking_academy_tool_launch.html.
...
www.cisco.com/edu/ - 22k · Cached - Similar pages

Internetworking Technology Handbook
home toc prev next glossary feedback search help Internetworking Technology Handbook.
Internetworking Basics. Introduction to LAN Protocols. ...
www.cisco.com/univercd/cc/td/doc/cisintwk/ito_doc/ - 14k - Aug 7, 2004 -
Cached - Similar pages

Cisco Security Advisory: Cisco IOS Interface Blocked by IPv4 ...
... problem. This advisory is available at http://**www.cisco.com**/warp/public/707/cisco-sa-
20030717-blocked.shtml. Affected Products. This ...
www.cisco.com/warp/public/ 707/cisco-sa-20030717-blocked shtml - 88k -
Cached - Similar pages

Cisco - Internet Security Advisories

This example only searches within the domain cisco.com. You
will want to check to see that all of your pages are being indexed
and that the text showing up next to the search results is close to
what you want it to be.

Besides Google, you will also want to try this with some other
search engines. The search terms are a little different for each
search engine. Here is a breakdown for the different search
engines to search within your domain.

Google: allinurl: www.cisco.com site:www.cisco.com
Altavista: +host:www.cisco.com +domain:com
Hotbot: domain:www.cisco.com
Teoma: site:www.cisco.com www.cisco.com
Lycos: site:www.cisco.com
Yahoo: www.cisco.com

Besides searching only within your domain, you will also want to checkout and see what other sites are linking to your pages and what pages they are linking to.

Some online sources may help you in checking your rankings. Some sites of interest are http://www.marketleap.com This site will check your link popularity and see how you are ranked for different search terms and how you compare against your competitors.

http://www.searchmechanics.com/look/look.htm   Search Mechanics allows you to put in your domain and do a search among different search engines to see how you are ranked without having to type in information into each search engine.

Checking for Dead Links

You need to occasionally check for dead links. This is important to do first after you are done creating your pages or websites and then once after the site has been uploaded to the server. Some HTML page programs may have link checkers built in.

However, if you get an error or your ftp program fails to upload some of your files, you may have some dead links. A great program I've found that can check for dead links and orphan files is Xenu's Link Sleuth. http://home.snafu.de/tilman/xenulink.html This program is free and does a great job of checking local links for dead links as well as internet links.

Tracking

You have spent a great deal of time optimizing your site and making it nice for your users. Now, you will want to make sure that your efforts are paying off. Tracking the traffic to your website is very important.

Free tracking programs are available as well as scripts that cost money. Most free scripts require that you simply cut and paste some JavaScript code into each of your pages.

When you have tracking setup, you will be able to see where your traffic is coming from. This is called referrers and will show you which sites are giving you most amount of traffic and what keywords people are typing in to access your page.

Below is a server-side tracking program called Urchin (http://www.urchin.com)

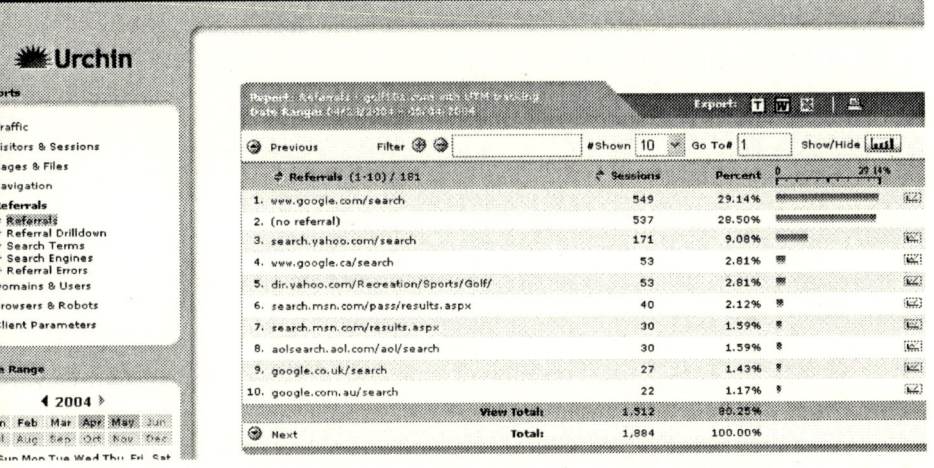

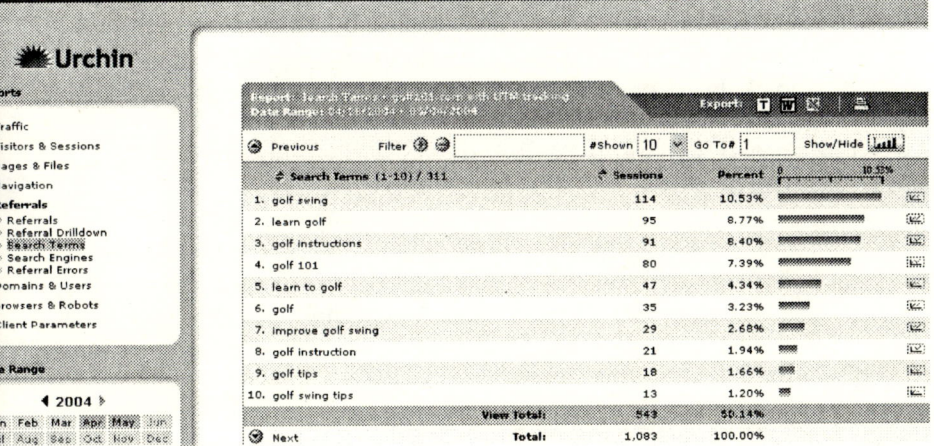

Also, you will be able to track how long people spend on your pages, what pages they access first, and what pages most people visit most. In addition you can find out what country they are from, what browser they are using and what screen resolution they are using.

This is an important step in seeing how well your search engine optimization is going. Periodically checking your stats will help to make sure you stay on top of search rankings.

There are two types of tracking you can do. You can do server-side log file tracking or 3rd party tracking. Server-side tracking is installed on your server and reads your log files and then compiles reports based on that. Server-side tracking will allow you to view things that you can't ordinarily do with 3rd party tracking such as the number of times images or multimedia content is viewed, the name of images viewed and more.

3rd party tracking requires that you cut & paste code into each page you want tracked such as html, php, or asp files.

Both have advantages and disadvantages. Server-Side tracking makes larger log files than normal which can use a lot of hard drive space on the server. Server-side tracking allows more things to be tracked, though.

3rd party tracking is fast and easy but may require that you keep image button at bottom of your screen. It also means you have to add code to each page. Server-side tracking does not always require this.

Army of Sites

As previously mentioned, links to your site are very important for improving your search engine rank. If you cannot get others to link your site, you may want to take another approach and create your own sites to link to your sites. Your sites must appear to be independent from one another.

In order to do this, you must have multiple sites which are each on separate IP addresses. They must be on different class C IP addresses. An example of this is below:

255.255.XXX.YYY

The X's must be different from your main site.

Further security tips are to have different domain name whois info for each of your domains and also, the name server or DNS server should be different as well.

There are different strategies that have been used with the army of sites strategy. The most obvious would be to have each site link to your main one. Of course this is too simplistic. You will also need these sites to link to one another and/or outside pages to make them appear more realistic.

Also, each doorway domain cannot be identical to one another. The layout of the page needs to be slightly different. The following could be different: (I have eliminated the obvious such as Page title and body text)

1. # of links on page
2. name of image
3. size of image
4. text / background color
5. table layout (# columns or rows)
6. page names

Most of these are pretty obvious similarities. In the past you could get away with creating template with same everything except page title, body text and link URLs. Today, it is more sophisticated. For example if Google indexes your pages and notices that domains 1, 2, 3 all link to site B and all have an image named logo1.jpg that is size 15KB, and the all have 10 links in each page this would definitely look suspicious to Google and could lower your ranking.

Page name is another one that is important. If a robot or doorway page generator makes a webpage, it may keep the same page name as the domain so that the page name is almost identical to the domain. An example of this would be something like: http://mp3world.com/mp3world.html If all of your domains follow a similar pattern, then this will definitely look like spam.

Some of these doorway pages worked extremely well in past. One such spammer was really killing Google with doorway pages. As a result, some big crackdowns took place.

One of these hacks that worked really well on Google was use of dynamic doorway pages. When you would refresh or reload the page, it would load a new set of keywords, text color and background color. By doing things like this, it may have appeared to Google that the website was always up to date and had unique content. As a result of these abuses, it is now difficult finding a page listed on Google that still does this. Yahoo still allows this, though. Below is an example of a dynamic doorway page.

5. Naked **Black Girls** 🔖

Naked **Black Girls** - pictures naked **black** women - naked **black** girl. ... WARNING
- Explicit adult www.naked-**black-girls**.us Warning! explicit photos of Naked **Black
Girls** You must read the following before ...
www.naked-black-girls.us/ - 5k - Cached - More pages from this site

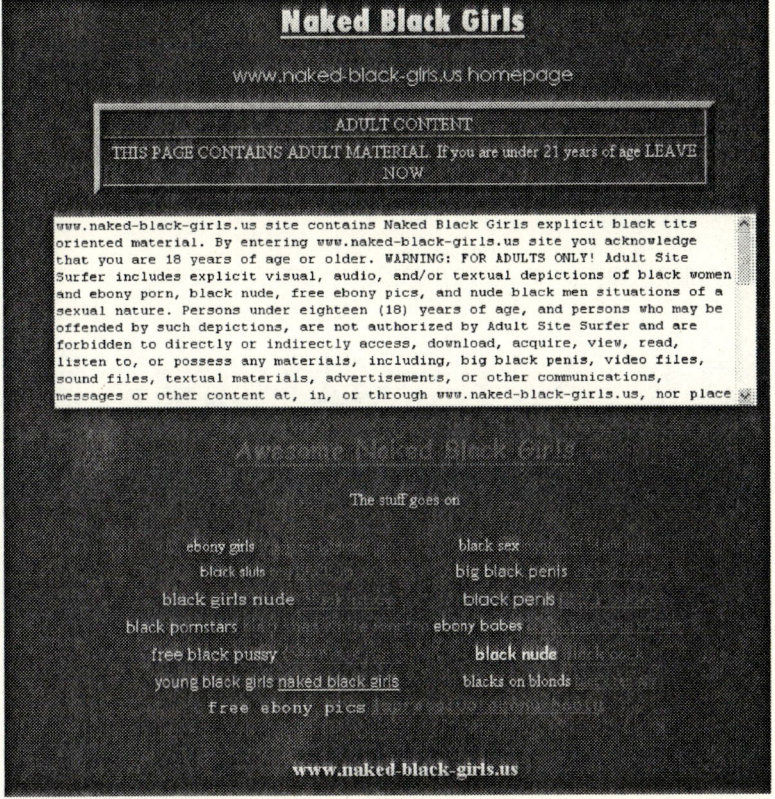

Upon refreshing the site, it will load new keywords and
background colors:

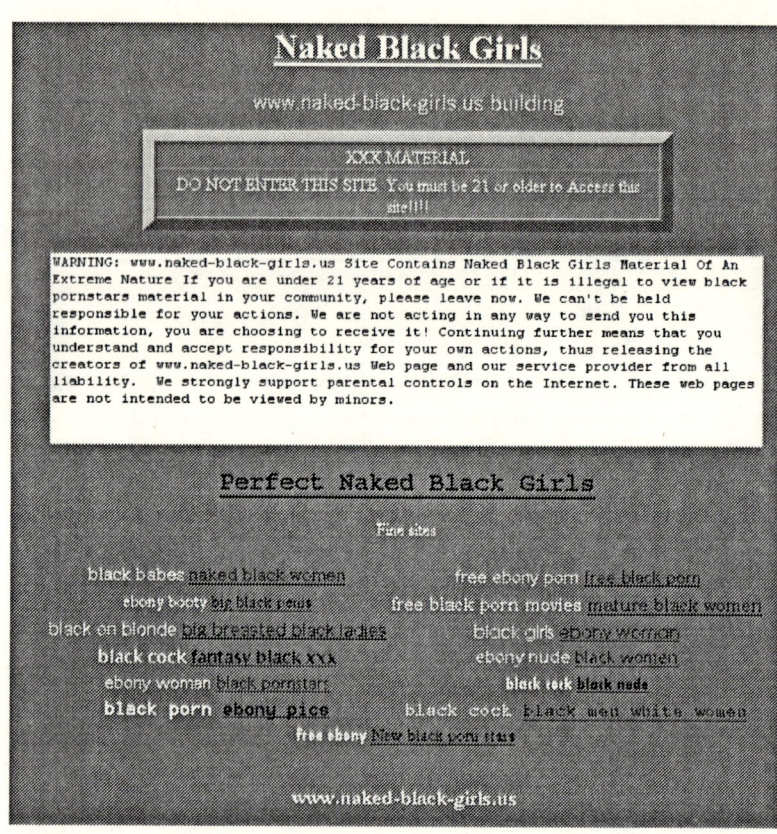

The army of sites strategy may not always be based on improving rank of one particular site. Some people don't have flagship sites but just doorway pages to other sites for which they are affiliates. The army of sites strategy can bring up sites that link to one another.

One important thing for this affiliate army of sites strategy is that you may not want to bring up the rank of the site that you are pointing to. If you are linking directly to your sponsor site with a normal link in your doorway pages, you may bring up the rank for your sponsor site for that link keyword.

The problem with this is that, it may bring up rank of your sponsor site above your site ratings. What some people may do to help with this problem is to have something like a php hyperlink which may not be indexed as well by Google. Or, a string in the URL may also make this less indexable by Google.

Another way of doing this is to have an image hyperlink to your sponsor site. This will make the link less important to Google.

By following some of these steps outlined above, the army of sites concept could significantly boost your search engine ratings and improve your traffic.

Things that should be banned by Google

Besides the obvious annoying things such as page re-directs, pop-ups, cloaking and fraudulent links, there are some other things that search engines will most likely ban in the future.

As mentioned when creating doorway pages, they should not be too similar to one another. If they are too similar to one another, Google should rank them as spam and lower rankings for sites or ban them.

Many sites are spamming Google with doorway pages that are obviously doorway pages created by software with little unique content.

When a page link in the webpage, the page title of linked page and page name all are named the same thing, this should be viewed as spam.

An example of this is to have a link on a page that says "free mp3s" then that page links to site with page title that says only "free mp3s" and then the page name of this page is also freemp3s.html.

One or two occurrences of this throughout a domain might be considered OK, but when this happens many times throughout a site it should most likely be banned.

Search Query Hack

One recent hack that you may have seen is the search query hack. You can spot it right away in the search results because of the URL. If you do a search for "mp3", you may see a site with the URL that ends in something like: /topsites.php?q=mp3 And, when you enter the site you may see other keyword links and they all have URLs similar to this, so the links may show /topsites.php?q=free+home+loan when you highlight it for free home loan link.

Most of these sites are partners of pay-per-click search engines. At the top of the site is usually a search bar where you can run a search. What it seems that they may be doing is using the search bar to capture typed in keywords from searches. Then, a link is made on the site with a query link to that keyword and custom page title.

By doing this, new keyword links can be made automatically without having to actually think of the keywords to use on the site. The internet surfer does all the work when they type in keywords and the script does the rest.

Search Engine Censorship

Both Yahoo and Google have censorship options in place for their search engine and image search sites.

Sign In - Yahoo! - Search Home - Help

Search Preferences

Click the Save Preferences button when you're done and we'll save your preferences to this computer. Sign in in to save your preferences to your Yahoo! ID.

[Save Preferences]

New Window	☐ Open search results in a new window when I click on them.
Number of Results	Display 20 results ▼ per page.
SafeSearch Filter	○ Strict - Filter out mature images and Web content ○ Moderate - Filter out mature images only ◉ Off - Do not filter search results Advisory: Yahoo! SafeSearch is designed to filter out explicit, adult-oriented content from Yahoo! Search results. However, Yahoo! cannot guarantee that all explicit content will be filtered out.
Language	Search only for pages written in: ◉ any language **or** ○ one or more of the following languages (select as many as you want).

☐ Arabic   ☐ German   ☐ Polish
☐ Bulgarian   ☐ Greek   ☐ Portuguese
☐ Catalan   ☐ Hebrew   ☐ Romanian
☐ Chinese (Simplified)   ☐ Hungarian   ☐ Russian
☐ Chinese (Traditional)   ☐ Icelandic   ☐ Serbian
☐ Croatian   ☐ Indonesian   ☐ Slovak
☐ Czech   ☐ Italian   ☐ Slovenian
☐ Danish   ☐ Japanese   ☐ Spanish
☐ Dutch   ☐ Korean   ☐ Swedish
☐ English   ☐ Latvian   ☐ Thai
☐ Estonian   ☐ Lithuanian   ☐ Turkish
☐ Finnish   ☐ Norwegian

Google Preferences

Prefere

Save your preferences when finished and return to search.

Global Preferences (changes apply to all Google services)

Interface Language	Display Google tips and messages in: English ▼ If you do not find your native language in the pulldown above, you can help Google create it through our Google in Your Language program.
Search Language	◉ Search for pages written in any language (Recommended). ○ Search only for pages written in these language(s):

☐ Arabic   ☐ English   ☐ Indonesian   ☐ Romanian
☐ Bulgarian   ☐ Estonian   ☐ Italian   ☐ Russian
☐ Catalan   ☐ Finnish   ☐ Japanese   ☐ Serbian
☐ Chinese (Simplified)   ☐ French   ☐ Korean   ☐ Slovak
☐ Chinese (Traditional)   ☐ German   ☐ Latvian   ☐ Slovenian
☐ Croatian   ☐ Greek   ☐ Lithuanian   ☐ Spanish
☐ Czech   ☐ Hebrew   ☐ Norwegian   ☐ Swedish
☐ Danish   ☐ Hungarian   ☐ Polish   ☐ Turkish
☐ Dutch   ☐ Icelandic   ☐ Portuguese

SafeSearch Filtering	Google's SafeSearch blocks web pages containing explicit sexual content from appearing in search results. ○ Use strict filtering (Filter both explicit text and explicit images) ○ Use moderate filtering (Filter explicit images only - default behavior) ◉ Do not filter my search results.
Number of Results	Google's default (10 results) provides the fastest results. Display 10 ▼ results per page.

As you can see both Yahoo and Google have similar search filters and censorship options. You can select searches based on language.

They both have what is called "safesearch" filtering. This is supposed to block pages with explicit sexual content from appearing in the search results. Three filtering options are available:

1. strict filtering (Filter both explicit text and explicit images)
2. moderate filtering (Filter explicit images only - default behavior)
3. do not filter my search results.

By default both of these search engines seem to default to some type of filtering such as #1 or #2. As a result of this, some sites will get removed from the search results. Many people may never even know to change these options from their default values.

A quick test is to pick a sexual word and do a search with the search filter set to #1. Then measure the number of search results you get back. Then try the same search but set it to #3 (no filtering). Then see how many more results you get back.

Besides this type of filtering, some search engines have filtered search results. Yahoo filters more than Google and filters certain keyword in both the search engine and the image search. Even with the search filter set to off, certain keywords return no results as a result of the censoring.

Google rarely filters results but has as a result of heavy publicity manually added some comments for one particular keyword.

Web   Images   Groups   News   Froogle   **more »**

Jew   [Search]   Advanced
                                                     Preference

---

Web

Offensive Search Results
www.google.com/explanation   We're disturbed about these results as well. Please read our

News results for **Jew** - View today's top stories

Who will be a **Jew**? - Jerusalem Post (subscription) - Aug 6, 2004

Jew - Wikipedia, the free encyclopedia
Jew. From Wikipedia, the free encyclopedia. A **Jew** is a follower of the Jewish faith (Judaism)
or a descendent of Jews, or both. ... [edit]. Who is a **Jew**? [edit]. ...
en.wikipedia.org/wiki/Jew - 101k - Aug 7, 2004 - Cached - Similar pages

Jew Watch
Jew Watch. Keeping ... Archived for Educational Purposes only Under USC Title 17 Section
107 by **Jew** Watch Library at jewwatch.com. *COPYRIGHT ...
www.jewwatch.com/ - 30k - Aug 7, 2004 - Cached - Similar pages

When doing a search the keyword "jew" Google has put an ad at the top of the page that says "Offensive Search Results." This goes to a Google page that describes that some sites in the search results may bring up unexpected results and anti-Semitic content sites.

Google further provides information and advice for searching and advices to search for "Judaism" and "Jewish people" if looking for information on Jewish people.

This came as a result of online petitions by people that wanted the word "jew" removed from Google. Google does not want to censor words from its search result so it put up the explanation page which gives information and further acts as a notice for others that want to censor words from Google.

http://news.com.com/2100-1038_3-5186012.html?tag=nefd.top
http://news.com.com/Google+protects+its+search+results/2100-1023_3-883558.html?tag=nl

The Google warning was not enough for some people. One group started a Google Bombing campaign to knock down the "Jewwatch" website from its top rank on Google.

http://www.jewschool.com/ This site got others to Google Bomb and try and drop down the Jewwatch site. Here is the info directly from the site:

"Wanna participate? Just drop <a href="http://en.wikipedia.org/wiki/Jew" target="_new">Jew</a> into your next blog post, or put it anywhere on your website. Be sure to spread this around to your mailing lists and your friends on IM too, so that we may actively engage in defining ourselves, as opposed to allowing others (with vicious intentions) to do so for us."

This is how Google bombing is done. As a result of this, Jewwatch was dropped down the search ranks on Google. Now, if you do a search for the word "jew" in Google you may notice that jewwatch is no longer #1 in the results.

Google Adwords

If you aren't getting the search engine results you want, you may want to look at paying for your results with a pay per click program like Google Adwords.

Some companies have become successful solely by using Google Adwords for advertising. Google Adwords is great in that you can get targeted traffic instantly and can shut it off instantly. Google gives you the flexibility you need to determine how you want to advertise.

Google Adwords allows your ads to appear when users type in certain search words in Google. In the screenshot below you can see the Google Adwords sponsored results on the right hand side of the page.

Google Adwords is a bidding system in which advertisers bid for keywords. The minimal cost per click for keywords is five cents per click. On more popular keywords, the cost per click may be as high as $4 or more. Google has set a maximum of $50 per click.

You will only pay for your ads when someone clicks on them. You are also free to set a daily budget. Once you've spent up to your daily budget, the ads will stop.

Google Adwords also allows you to pause and delete ad campaigns.

Once you have decided some of the keywords you want to use, you may use Google's keyword recommendation tool to create new related keywords.

If your keywords are too broad, it may increase your impressions and click leading to lower ROI (return on investment). Using specific, more relevant keywords can increase your ROI saving you money.

You will also want to see an estimate of where you will appear in rank based on the amount of money you are willing to pay per keyword. If you aren't willing to pay enough, your ad will appear near the bottom of the page which may lead to fewer people clicking on the ad.

https://adwords.google.com/select/library/index.html

Conclusion

I've shown you some of the hacks used on Google. By taking some of the steps recommended in this book, you should see your rank with Google improve. I hope you have enjoyed this book.

Printed in the United States
23820LVS00001B/252